The Spelling Teacher's Handbook

JO PHENIX

Pembroke Publishers Limited

KH

Other Books by Jo Phenix

The Spelling Teacher's Book
of Lists
Teaching the Skills
Teaching Writing

Spelling Instruction That
Makes Sense (with
Doreen Scott-Dunne)
Spelling for Parents (with
Doreen Scott-Dunne)

© 2001 Folens Limited

Pembroke Publishers
538 Hood Road
Markham, Ontario, Canada L3R 3K9
www.pembrokepublishers.com

Distributed in the U.S. by Stenhouse Publishers
477 Congress Street
Portland, ME 04101
www.stenhouse.com

This edition is adapted from a book written by Jo Phenix and first
published by Folens Limited (UK).
E-mail: folens@folens.com

National Library of Canada Cataloguing in Publication Data

Phenix, Jo
   The spelling teacher's handbook

ISBN 1-55138-138-9

   1. English language—Orthography and spelling—Study and
teaching (Elementary) I. Title.

LB1574.P554 2001   372.63'2   C2001-901954-8

Editors: Karen Westall, Laura Edlund, Lori Burak
Layout artist: Suzanne Ward, Jay Tee Graphics
Illustrations: Debbie Riviere
Cover Design: John Zehethofer

Printed and bound in Canada
9 8 7 6 5 4 3 2 1

9/19/06

Contents

Understanding spelling

The skills of spelling

English spelling in North America reflects the histories of both the British Isles and this continent. In the British Isles, a succession of invasions by different language speakers created a hybrid that many linguists classify as a pidgin tongue. The language that the printing press fixed on the page for us contains elements of many languages, predominantly Latin (although this influence largely disappeared in the post-Roman period and is now evident in English-from-French words), Anglo-Saxon, Norse and French. When English speakers came to North America as explorers and settlers, the language adapted to its various new settings, adopted words from Native North American languages, and evolved regionally. Around the globe, English speakers have never been slow to adopt words from any language they have come into contact with.

Because of this checkered background, we have come to think of English as a language devoid of logic and pattern, and its spelling as often random and confusing. Even what we call "spelling rules" always seem to have exceptions.

Order out of chaos

To unravel the maze of spelling for children, we need to show them that there is far more logic than they might at first recognize. Our spelling is, in fact, full of patterns that we can identify and use to become proficient spellers.

Learning the real skills of spelling has little to do with memorizing lists of words. A good speller is not necessarily a person with a good memory, but one who understands the patterns of English and can use them to construct words as they are needed.

Effective spelling instruction must focus on patterns and word-building strategies that children can use in their own writing. The teaching of spelling should also be closely linked to the teaching of handwriting since the experienced writer often "feels" he or she may have made an error before seeing it. We can learn much by looking at the five stages that children go through on the road to becoming effective at spelling.

Stages of development in learning to spell

Pre-phonetic

Children attempt a message that may be a mixture of pictures, letter shapes or signs. The meaning can very often only be interpreted by the writer.

Characteristics
✔ Randomly uses both conventional and invented symbols.
✔ Repeats known symbols.
✔ Mixes upper and lower case symbols.
✔ Writing is translatable only by the writer.

Moving the child forward
✔ Develop the child's interest and attention to print.
✔ Encourage the child to "hold" the message.
✔ Provide a translation *after* the child has written.
✔ Draw attention to and demonstrate written messages, vocalizing sounds, rhymes and patterns.
✔ Introduce alphabetic names and initial sounds.

Semi-phonetic

The picture begins to be separated from the message. The message often contains pictograms and letter-like shapes. Children will often use upper case letters, especially from their own names. One symbol often symbolizes a whole sentence.

Characteristics
✔ Attempts to match letters or symbols to sounds.
✔ Often uses letter names to represent sounds.
✔ Begins to orient letters and words left to right.
✔ Begins to distinguish strong consonant sounds; not many vowels.

Moving the child forward
✔ Encourage the "try-it!" approach and the use of "invented" or "temporary" spelling.
✔ Reinforce knowledge of letter sounds, names and alphabetical order.
✔ Vocalize sounds when demonstrating spelling and encourage children to listen for sounds and vocalize as they spell.
✔ Begin to split words into beginning, middle and end.
✔ Direct attention to common words in the classroom and environment for copying.
✔ Begin banks of high-frequency and "key" words.

Phonetic

The message contains some symbols that represent sounds. The sounds are usually very familiar, such as letters from a name or from a word that the child uses frequently. Familiar letters are often included as capitals.

Characteristics
✔ Uses known sounds to write words.
✔ Writing becomes readable by others.
✔ Becomes aware of word boundaries and leaves spaces (not always in the conventional place).
✔ Pronunciation plays a large part in the spelling of words.
✔ Often omits nasal consonants.
✔ If in doubt, often puts extra letters in to cover gaps in knowledge.

Moving the child forward
✔ Begin to record words in alphabetical lists.
✔ Encourage syllabification of words.
✔ Focus on the visual features, onsets, rime patterns, letter strings, etc.
✔ Encourage children to make analogies when spelling.
✔ Work on the different ways of representing sounds, e.g., long vowels.
✔ Build lists of words with similar spelling patterns.

Transitional to visual

Children may stay in this stage for some time; indeed it is where many "stick." They should be moving from a phonic to a visual approach, starting to recognize if a word "looks right." They can often learn this by proofreading the work of others. They should show evidence of an increasing bank of known words and some spelling should now be "automatic." Many children may need to practise frequently-used words to the point of "overlearning." They may still use an inappropriate but logical pattern or revert to phonic strategies.

Characteristics
✔ Uses strategies other than phonic and is able to make analogies.
✔ Majority of letters in words are correct but not necessarily in correct sequence.
✔ Includes a vowel in every syllable.
✔ May over-generalize on a rule, e.g., final e (*biye* for *buy*).
✔ Spells correctly more frequently-used words.
✔ May develop word "blocks" for specific words, e.g., *sentance*.
✔ Begins to use unvoiced or silent letters, e.g., *finking* instead of *fickig* for *thinking*.

Moving the child forward
✔ Emphasize the role of "drafting" in writing and spelling.
✔ Encourage children to proofread and check each other's work.
✔ Extend children's range of vocabulary.
✔ Focus on the meaning of words to examine root words and derivatives.
✔ Develop children's research strategies and use of dictionaries, thesauruses, word lists and spellcheckers.
✔ Encourage children to discuss with others the strategies they use when spelling.

Conventional or mature

If children have been encouraged to observe print around them and to build up their visual memory of words encountered in their reading, sentence and word work, these words should begin to appear in their writing. There will be some reliance on phonetic spelling and children should be praised for what they get nearly right and encouraged to check spellings (perhaps with a partner) before presenting their work. Class and group work should be aimed at both building a spelling vocabulary of "key words" and learning the patterns and letter strings common to English. At this stage, children should be able to "invent" a word using conventional spelling patterns, e.g., *dracularess*.

Characteristics
- ✔ Uses a full range of strategies – phonic, visual, morphemic, conventional – to spell words.
- ✔ Makes analogies from known spelling patterns.
- ✔ Knows a large bank of "sight" words.
- ✔ Tries alternatives to see which "look and feel right."
- ✔ Effectively uses spelling resources and reference books.
- ✔ Recognizes incorrect spelling.
- ✔ Has the confidence to try new and difficult words.

Moving the child forward
- ✔ Further develop use of drafting, proofreading and editing skills.
- ✔ Explore and examine the functions and meanings of words and how these affect spelling.
- ✔ Investigate the origins of words and the history of spelling systems.
- ✔ Develop the ability to spell correctly when writing at speed.
- ✔ Extend knowledge and use of appropriate reference sources.
- ✔ Foster an interest and enjoyment in word play and word collection and exploration.

(This material is based on the stages originally identified by R. Gentry in An Analysis of Developmental Spelling, *The Reading Teacher*, 36(2), 1982.)

A sequence of spelling development

A child's first encounter with written language is usually in picture books. Children's first realization that the language they are hearing someone read aloud is represented by the print, rather than by the pictures, is one of the intellectual breakthroughs of literacy. In early writing, children often use pictograms such as smiley or sad faces, hearts to say "I Love You!" and xxx for kisses. This demonstrates that they understand the importance of writing as a means of sending a message.

Once children recognize the function of print, they can move on to learning the alphabet and naming the letters. It is useful to remember this natural pattern for learning: if children first understand what something means, and what it is for, they can more easily learn how to use it. To teach spelling effectively, we must put meaning first.

Spelling development usually follows a sequence like the following:

1. Letter names

Can you relate the names of these letters to the following sentence?

    O   I C U   F N   N E N R G
    Oh, I see you haven't any energy.

Children can use the similarity of letter names to actual words in order to write down much of their own language. When children try to write using strings of apparently random letters, it is a sign that they have learned the connection between letters and language.

Translation: hedgehog, cucumbers, wire netting.

2. Phonics

Consonants

The next step in literacy comes when children learn that letters represent sounds. This is the time when phonics instruction is vitally important. They learn consonant sounds first, because they are easier to hear and distinguish from one another. Writing may still appear to be strings of letters, but the children will be attempting to represent the sounds they hear.

wder bodol
rag
food
bugs
einses
Toes
guvs
LVLuve
gale

Benjamin made a list of things he needed to care for his pet hedgehog, Cedar. Items on the list are:

water bottle
rag
food
bugs
insects
toys
gloves
love
cage

Vowels

As the children learn more about phonics, they learn to listen also for vowel sounds. At first, they will use vowel names; then they will learn rhyming patterns for writing vowel syllables.

Care of my pet hedgehog.

As we look at the children's writing at this phonetic stage, we can assess what they know and what they have not yet learned.

Then we played baseball
with my friend
Then we played football
with my friend
Then we had a race
with my friend

Colleen, age 5

What does Colleen know about spelling?
✔ She uses consonant sounds correctly most of the time.
✔ She represents every syllable of every word.
✔ She knows some sight words: *my, we.*
✔ She may have recognized *le* as a typical word ending.
✔ She uses spaces between words, therefore understands what a word is.

What does Colleen not yet know?
✔ Long-vowel patterns. She uses vowel names to represent vowel sounds: *pad, basble, ras.*
✔ Short-vowel patterns. She uses the closest vowel name she can find to represent short-vowel sounds: *a* in *then, e* in *with.*
✔ Consonant combination *th.* She uses a reversed *z,* which is the closest letter-name match she can find.

The next step in learning for Colleen will be short-vowel rhyming patterns, followed by long-vowel patterns.

3. Spelling patterns

To progress from phonetic spelling to standard spelling, the children need to learn spelling patterns. These fall into four main groups:

✔ Sound patterns, in which similar sounds are represented by the same groups of letters:

<u>spl</u>at, <u>spl</u>ash, <u>spl</u>inter   r<u>ough</u>, t<u>ough</u>, en<u>ough</u>

✔ Function patterns, in which spelling is influenced by the way a word is used:

part<u>ed</u>, danc<u>ed</u>

Although pronunciation may change, the spelling of the past-tense marker remains the same.

dog<u>s</u>, cat<u>s</u>

Although pronunciation changes, the regular plural ending is always *s*.

✔ Meaning patterns, which connect words according to their meaning and origin.

<u>please</u>, <u>pleas</u>ant, dis<u>please</u>, <u>pleas</u>ure

Although pronunciation changes, the spelling of the root remains the same.

In words derived from French, *ch* sounds like *sh*.

chandelier, chemise, chamois, chef

In words derived from Greek, *ch* sounds like *k*.

chorus, choir, chemist

✔ Word-building patterns, which enable children to use the knowledge of the other three patterns in order to build words.

Knowledge of roots, prefixes and suffixes — and what they mean, the function they serve, and how to join them together — will enable children to make reasonable attempts to write new words.

4. Spelling by analogy

Because English spelling reflects patterns from many different languages, there is a large number of patterns to learn. As our vocabularies grow, we can fit new words into the patterns we know. To spell a word we have never written before, or perhaps never seen before, we think of other words with which it might match. This spelling-by-analogy is a strategy successful spellers use throughout their lives. It will not eliminate spelling errors, but it does give a writer a reasonable chance of figuring out a word's spelling.

---

medicine or medisine?

Think of other words in this pattern: *medical*   *medication*

                 medicate *paramedic*

Now you can predict that *c* will be the right choice.

If in addition you know that the word comes from French, you will predict that *cine* is the more likely spelling.

What skills should we teach?

Teaching the patterns that will enable children to construct the words they need will demonstrate that spelling is not a guessing game. It is a problem-solving activity with its own logic and predictability. Letter combinations, roots, prefixes and suffixes form the building blocks of words. The more children know about the parts of words, and what they mean and how they join together, the better spellers they will be.

Even more important, once children know that they have strategies to use and a reasonable chance of success, they can become more confident to try new words.

> The most severe spelling problem children can have does not concern the number of spelling errors they make. The greatest problem comes when a child draws the conclusion that being a poor speller is the same as being a poor writer.

Writing is the only purpose for spelling. When spelling forms a barrier between children and their writing, this is a spelling disability.

Three aspects of spelling learning

We can see spelling instruction as a three-part focus:

Attitude

Spelling is not boring slug-work. Nor is it a necessary evil of the writing process. Words are interesting and worthy of study. We want children to have a positive attitude towards spelling and understand its place in the writing process.

Knowledge

Facts and information about words will provide the raw materials with which to build words. Throughout their lives, children will continue to add to this store of knowledge.

Skills

Through frequency of use, children will develop an ability to use the information they have in order to construct words as they are needed.

Organizing a spelling classroom

Creating a climate for spelling learning

Most people make spelling mistakes, and it is in the nature of our society to regard errors as signs of carelessness, illiteracy and poor teaching methods. Even adults who are themselves poor spellers often define "good teaching" as "the way it was done when I went to school." As spelling is one of the more visible aspects of writing, it may be a first focus for comment. Parents often expect their young children to be able to write without making errors, not recognizing that, with such a complex spelling system, it will take many years for their children to learn enough even to come close to standard spelling.

Many children are afraid of making spelling mistakes. This fear may be the result of criticism, poor test results, losing marks for spelling, laborious corrections or frustration in trying and failing to remember words. Fear of making spelling mistakes can lead children to use strategies that work very successfully to cut down errors but restrict writing.

Confident versus safe

Confident spellers

Try any word within their speaking vocabularies.

Understand that making mistakes is part of learning to write.

Make their best attempt, then check the spelling later.

Understand the link between letter and sound patterns, even before they have mastered them.

Write as much or as little as time and interest allows, not as much as their spelling allows.

Make analogies and generalizations from words they already know.

Are prepared to "play" with words.

Have a range of different strategies using clues from different spelling patterns.

"Safe" spellers

Use easy words they know how to spell – write *big* rather than *enormous*.

Often seem to spell well because they don't attempt new words.

Find proofreading and checking a traumatic task.

Often spell the same word differently within the same piece of writing.

Write as little as possible, and often indulge in time-filling and avoidance behavior to cover lack of confidence.

Are unable to make analogies and generalizations.

Are less likely to experiment and play with words.

Tend to rely on one strategy all the time. Have poor sight-word vocabularies, and resort to sounding out high-frequency words.

If we look at the writing of Benjamin, we can see that as early as 6 years old he is a confident writer:

I am going to Disney World for my summer vacation. I am going on the Tower of Terror. My family is going to the Disney character breakfast.

✔ He writes about what he will see, not what he can spell.
✔ He is not frightened to attempt *Disney* and uses his phonic knowledge to make a very logical attempt.
✔ He is able to split words into segments and attempt each part: *vacation, summer.*
✔ He has vocalized the word *summer* and his attempt reflects his pronunciation.
✔ He knows some short-vowel sounds: *sumr.*
✔ He is beginning to experiment with long-vowel sounds and although he often reverts to using letter names, this does not put him off attempting a word.
✔ He knows several high-frequency words: *of, for, the, on, going.*
✔ He is confident in his writing and spelling.

Key points to encourage confidence in spelling

✔ Demonstrate the strategies you use as an adult when spelling words.

✔ Know what stage of spelling development the children are at and what will be necessary to move them forward.

✔ In SHARED sessions, encourage all the children to volunteer help in spelling and praise attempts, however unconventional.

✔ In GUIDED sessions, work closely with groups to attempt words that they will need to use or that will extend their vocabulary.

✔ Encourage children to use their eyes, ears, hands, minds — and their knowledge about language.

✔ Encourage children to talk about their spelling strategies as they write.

✔ Allow strategies using "draft" or "temporary" spellings: clxxd, croc-d–l, etc.; examining these attempts can often reveal a rule imperfectly understood.

✔ Encourage children to use the symbol "sp" in their own writing to indicate a word they wish to check later.

✔ Encourage children to discuss their spelling with a partner or their group and to use as many alternative strategies as they can before approaching you.

✔ Allow them to copy words or phrases that they see around them in the classroom and in the environment, but always with a "look, say, cover, write, check" approach (for further details, see p. 60).

✔ Teach each stage of the above approach and explain why it is important. Children need to understand how words are constructed for them to be stored in long-term memory.

✔ Encourage them to practise key and high-frequency words with their eyes closed. This helps them to feel the movements involved in forming the letters.

✔ As soon as possible, teach children to practise spellings in cursive writing so that the movement is continuous.

✔ Emphasize and re-emphasize that spelling is part of editing and that incorrect spelling in initial drafts is perfectly acceptable.

✔ When assessing spelling, praise what has been spelled correctly, rather than counting errors. Look for growth in relation to each child's ability and past performance.

The reading – writing connection

The first step towards teaching children how to produce writing of their own is to demonstrate the purposes reading and writing serve. Children need to know not only that literacy is important to participate fully in life, but also that it can fulfil personal purposes for them.

The best atmosphere in which to learn any of the skills of literacy is one in which reading and writing are valued, used for real purposes, studied and practised.

Some people have believed that if children do enough reading and writing, the learning of skills will take care of itself; that children will pick up all the information they need during reading and writing activities. In some cases, this does happen; some children seem to learn about spelling and grammar spontaneously without much direct teaching. For many children, though, this kind of learning does not happen, and in most cases we can help in the learning. In a complete and balanced classroom program, regular practice and planned instruction will operate side by side.

The same model for teaching holds true in both reading and writing:

✔ Engage the children in daily reading and writing for real purposes. This will create a need for learning the skills in order that the job is done well.
✔ Teach the children the skills they need to help them to become more proficient. This in turn will make reading and writing tasks more successful and more satisfying. There is nothing more motivating for further learning than success.

Risk-taking

Children cannot learn to spell before they start to write; throughout their lives, their ability to spell will always lag behind their vocabulary. If we want improvement in both spelling and in composition, we must establish a risk-free environment in which children can use the best knowledge they have to write using every word in their speaking vocabulary.

Strategies to encourage risk-taking

✔ Establish a "writers' workshop" atmosphere. This will help children to learn that writing is moulded into shape, rather than springing full-blown into a finished form. Working towards correct spellings is one part of this process.

OFFICIAL SPELLCHECKERS

✔ Allow plenty of time for children to proofread and correct, before they are held accountable for spelling errors. Final draft is the time to assess spelling competence. It is often helpful if children are encouraged to work with a partner when editing their writing before presentation or marking. Children find it much easier to proofread the work of others and this helps to train them to spot errors.

✔ Reward failed attempts to spell difficult words. You want children to keep trying, not be afraid to use new words.

✔ Do not regard spelling errors as signs of carelessness or laziness. They are more likely to be signs that a child has not yet internalized a pattern. Many good spellers make errors in first-draft writing because they are concentrating on what they have to say, or writing very quickly.

✔ Use spelling errors as opportunities to assess what children know and do not know. Explain to the children why their words are wrong and which spelling concept they did not know.

✔ Respond to what children do correctly, as well as to what they do wrong. No one can get a word completely wrong; if you have every letter wrong, you have written a different word. An error is usually one letter or syllable, a word ending, a vowel combination, or a doubled letter, and represents a spelling concept or pattern. Point out which parts are correct before explaining the error.

✔ Do not expect children to be able to proofread for patterns they have not yet learned. Their speaking vocabulary will always exceed their ability to spell.

✔ Provide all the help children need to bring their writing to final-draft stage. Even poor spellers deserve to have their writing displayed and published.

✔ Encourage children to use tape-recorders to compose orally. This will enable them to use the best language they can, without considering whether or not they can spell the words. They can then transcribe their own language, or have a scribe do it for them. Once children know how well and how much they can compose, few of them are satisfied with lesser efforts. It will also give you a chance to assess their composing ability separately from their skill in transcription.

✔ Encourage even older children to compose by drawing a series of pictures. They can then write accompanying text for each picture, or use a tape-recorder as in the example above. This will break down the task of composing and writing into smaller units and allow children to focus on composing and spelling one at a time.

✔ Make a record, keeping a list of patterns and concepts each child knows and uses. Whatever the level of achievement, each child can have a growing list.

Planning instruction

If we are to help our children to become more proficient in spelling, we must plan our instruction around the three prerequisites for learning anything:

✔ Purpose
✔ Information
✔ Practice

Purpose

Writing provides the only valid purpose for learning to spell. A classroom that provides opportunities for many different kinds of writing will create a need for learning to spell.

In order to write effectively and efficiently, children need two different kinds of spelling skill. They will learn which one is appropriate as they use the drafting process in their writing.

✔ Try-it! spelling
✔ Correct spelling

Try-it! spelling

Children need to be able to write quickly and freely without giving spelling undue thought. Although this may result in many spelling mistakes, it is intended for first-draft writing and for quick, personal jottings, not for public scrutiny. A reasonable spelling facility enables children to get their ideas and language down on paper quickly and to focus on the composing aspects of writing first.

Strategies to encourage try-it! spelling

✔ Teach the "try-it!" strategy. If children are not sure of a spelling, they should try it, make their best attempt and mark the word to check later. You can establish a "try-it!" symbol, such as the symbol TI. Establish the principle that if the children write this beside a word, they will not be penalized or criticized for a misspelling, as long as they check it at the appropriate time. TI can be a licence to experiment, a "get out of jail free" card. As you look at their attempts, you can get information about the kinds of thinking children do as they try to form words. Do they sound it out phonetically? Are they trying to use a spelling pattern? Do they represent all the syllables? Is their attempt a possible or an impossible spelling?

✔ Avoid comments, either verbal or written, on spelling during first-draft writing. Whenever you mention spelling, even to praise, you are sending the message that spelling is something that the child should be thinking about at this time.

✔ From time to time, give children a speed-writing task. Assign a topic and ask them to write for three minutes. At the end of the three minutes, they are to count how many words they have written. The children can record their own score and try to beat it next time. Do not read this writing; it is only to give the children practice in writing quickly without thinking about spelling or neatness.

✔ Encourage children to cross out, rather than trying to erase spelling errors. Do this yourself when you write on the board and need to change a word or phrase. This will foster the notion that at this time speed is important, rather than neatness.

✔ Model these strategies when you write on the board, or while the children are watching. They should see that when you write it is not always right first time.

✔ Provide scrap paper, or an exercise book in which no marks or comments are recorded, for first-draft writing and quick notes. This can then become a risk-free workplace in which children can focus on getting their thoughts and language down on paper. Children will not be so anxious about messing up writing that will remain totally private.

Correct spelling

Children need to know how to produce correct spellings, and when and why this is important. For this, it is not enough just to write. It is of little importance if we misspell words on a shopping list, or when writing the first draft of a story. To provide real purpose for correct spelling, the writing must be intended for another person to read. Then we learn that if our spelling is incorrect, we will make a poor impression. For writing to be a significant factor in learning to spell, the writer must be writing for a real audience. No one wants to look silly in print.

Strategies to encourage correct spelling

✔ Provide many opportunities for children to write for audiences both within and outside the classroom.

✔ Teach children that correct spelling, neat handwriting and an attractive presentation are courtesies you pay to your reader. You want to make reading your writing an easy and pleasant experience. If their work is too messy and untidy for you to want to read, say so. Real audience feedback is a good way to learn what is important.

✔ Teach children that correcting their spelling is like combing their hair when they are going to have their photograph taken, cleaning the house when visitors are coming, or putting on their best clothes for a special occasion. Sometimes writing has a public face, and there are times when we all want to look our best. Analogies like these may help children to understand how much time and effort they should put into making their writing correct and attractive.

✔ Do not display or publish work with spelling mistakes. Children should know that the final draft is the public face of writing and should be as correct and attractive as they can make it.

✔ Do not expect children to proofread and correct every piece of writing. This will foster the notion that spelling is equally important in every writing task, and will work against them learning when spelling really matters.

✔ Give children all the help that they need to proofread and correct spellings for final-draft writing.

✔ Make good use of short dictation practice as an aid to checking how well children are progressing with high-frequency words or with particular spelling patterns or rules. It is much better to deliver a dictation in sentence or paragraph form rather than the isolated words of a spelling test, as this enables children to use their knowledge of context to help them. Give the dictation in the same "try-it!" manner as normal writing, and pitch it at or slightly above the children's level. This might make it more suitable for a group GUIDED activity than a whole class activity. With young children, you might begin with three or four short sentences of regular phonic or high-frequency words. At first, give the children as much time as they need. When the children have had some practice, you could use this occasionally as a speed test. The children can correct their own attempts, perhaps working with a partner, and should only be graded against their own progress.

These first attempts can reveal very useful diagnostic information about the main strategies that the children use, words that are automatic for them, and any persistent errors. They can be particularly helpful in stretching "safe" spellers to attempt words that they might avoid in their personal writing, thus revealing strengths and gaps in their knowledge. Dictation, if it focuses on high-frequency or taught vocabulary, can teach children that spelling "sight words" correctly at the first attempt saves time in the long term and makes writing much easier.

Children need to know which kind of spelling is appropriate to any writing task. To help them to learn this, we must be very consistent in the way we set expectations and respond to spelling errors, not only from lesson to lesson, and from teacher to teacher, but throughout the children's school career. If children understand the purpose of spelling, and of the drafting process, they should never need to ask, "Does spelling count?"

Information

The information that children need is two-fold:

✔ The knowledge that spelling is a thinking activity
✔ Specific information about words

A thinking activity

Children need to know that spelling is a thinking, not a memorizing, activity. "Why?" is often as important a question in spelling as "how?" Understanding why words are spelled the way they are can help children to find patterns, make logical connections and develop strategies for making reasonable predictions about words. The more children know about the usage, history and derivations of words, the better spelling choices they will make.

> Why does *debt* have a silent *b*? The *b* was deliberately put into this word to reflect its origin in the Latin *debitum*.
>
> debt   debit   debenture
>
> Samuel Johnson, writer of the first major English dictionary, believed it important that spelling reflect the meaning of words, rather than the sound. Look back to page 10 to see how knowing a word's language of origin can help predict its spelling.

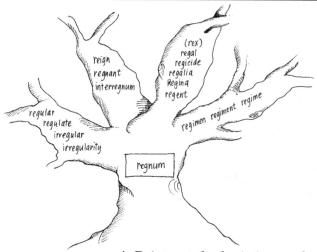

Why does *reign* have a silent *g*? From the Latin *regnum*, meaning rule or govern.

Strategies to encourage thinking

✔ Point out the logic in words that the children are writing. This will demonstrate for them how they can "spell by analogy," and work out possible spellings.

"The first sound is the same as in your name. Which letter should you use?"

"Can you think of another word that rhymes with *dog*? How would you spell it?"

"*Revise* and *revision* have the same root; it means "to see." Notice that even though the pronunciation is different, the spelling is the same. Which other words have the same root as these?"

✔ Explain the origins of words.

Because is a short form for three words (*be the cause*). This can help children to spell the second syllable correctly.

Tomorrow used to be *on the morrow*. This can help children to remember which letter is doubled and which is not.

When children are fascinated by words and their origins, when they become engaged in the task of generating spellings as children learning to talk are engaged in generating language, then we will know that they understand spelling as a cognitive process.

Specific information   At the same time as children are learning to think logically about words, we can give them specific information about words.

Strategies for gaining information

✔ Collect and categorize words. Sorting words according to spelling patterns will not only help children to recognize patterns, but will also teach them to expect and look for patterns.

✔ Investigate words. Find out their language of origin, their meanings, their usages, their abbreviations, their synonyms, antonyms and rhymes. This will not only raise children's interest in words, but demonstrate how words are linked.

✔ Analyse words. Find a word's root, prefixes and suffixes. Note how these parts are joined together.

✔ Help children to build a store of sight words. These might be high-frequency words, or words personal to each child. Frequency of use is the best way for children to learn these words.

✔ Teach children to use reference materials, so that they can find the words they need.

Practice

Learning to spell is largely a matter of pattern recognition. Once we have identified a pattern, we make a generalization: this kind of word is built in this kind of way. It is these generalizations that allow us to make reasonable predictions about how a word is most likely to be spelled.

Some people recognize and use patterns easily, often without being aware that they are doing so. These people learn to spell early, subconsciously assimilating information about words as they read, and are reasonably good spellers all their lives. Other people see words as individual entities, and do not recognize how they are linked to one another.

Seeing words grouped according to spelling patterns will help children to recognize the patterns. Building words according to these patterns will show children how to use them to spell. Using words frequently will help to make the patterns, and hence the words, automatic.

Some children will need many repetitions of patterns to be able to make the generalizations necessary for them to become competent spellers.

Strategies for providing practice

✔ Build words. Using the same pattern to build many words will help children to internalize the pattern and show them how they can use the pattern to spell new words for their writing.

✔ Play with words. Use crosswords, word searches and word games. Investigate palindromes and acronyms. Use alliteration. These all draw attention to ways in which words are constructed.

✔ Proofread regularly. It is a learned skill.

✔ Write many times a day for different purposes. Frequency of use is the best way to learn patterns, sight words and strategies.

Spelling across the curriculum

It is a truism that every teacher is a teacher of English. This also means that every teacher is a teacher of spelling. While some principles apply in every subject, different subject disciplines can also make different contributions to a child's spelling learning. Children and their parents should receive a consistent message about what is important, and about how they should be thinking about spelling.

It is primarily the English teacher's task to build up children's knowledge of spelling patterns and concepts and to provide the practice time necessary for children to become skilled at using this information. The methodology used in English time should be carried through in other subject areas. It is very confusing for children to learn a drafting approach to writing in English, then lose marks for spelling in a first-draft history report. Similarly, when children are learning spelling as a word-constructing activity, they should not at other times be expected to memorize lists of words for a test.

It is a good idea to establish some guidelines for teaching spelling and for responding to spelling errors in children's writing. These can be used in different subjects and by different teachers.

Sample guidelines

✔ Risk-taking should be supported at all times. Children doing their best is all we expect if they run a race or paint a picture; it should be acceptable in spelling too.

✔ The drafting process should be used for all writing. If writing stays in first-draft form, it should be evaluated as such.

✔ Children should not be penalized for spelling errors unless they have had ample time for proofreading and correcting, and been given all the help they need.

✔ Each subject teacher can teach subject-specific vocabulary and spellings. These should be taught by grouping words into patterns and word families, and through investigation of their origins, roots, meanings, derivations and so on — not by rote memorization.

✔ Children can keep personal reference lists of theme words, subject-specific words, words they have difficulty with, high-frequency words and so on. They could do this in a spelling journal they keep with them throughout the day.

Chapter 3

Planning spelling lessons

Objectives

The prime objective of a spelling lesson is to enable children to understand words, think about them logically and make connections among them so that they can build the words they need for their writing. It is essential to focus on long-term learning, rather than short-term memory. This long-term learning will result when children gain an understanding of the way in which words are constructed, and the way they link with one another.

All the words used in a spelling lesson should have a logical spelling connection. Focus on only one pattern at a time. It does not matter how many or how few words go together; a spelling pattern may have five words or a hundred words. Remember, the children are not learning the words, but the patterns.

Lists of words play an important part in spelling lessons. However, they are not lists of words to learn, but lists of words to illustrate patterns. If children internalize a pattern, they do not need to remember the words – they can reconstruct them whenever they need them. Not only that, they can use the pattern to spell correctly similar words they meet in the future. A pattern that they learn in class today can help them to spell words not yet in their speaking vocabularies. A spelling pattern lasts forever.

A four-step model for instruction

A spelling lesson can be a four-step process:

Step 1 Select patterns or rules that fit with a theme or topic you are working on, and collect example words.

Step 2 Sort the words according to the spelling patterns involved.

Step 3 Examine the lists of words and make generalizations about why they are different.

Step 4 Use the pattern to build new words.

Sample spelling lesson

Spelling focus: Plural patterns

Time span: 3–4 days

Whole class work (10 minutes)

On an overhead transparency, list plural words from the first three pages of Chapter 1 of *Alice in Wonderland*:

pictures daisies bookshelves conversations

Children contribute other plural words. Start with objects around the room. Then suggest themes – animals, fruit.

Group work – groups of four (10 minutes)

Duplicate copies of the transparency list, one for each group.
Children cut apart the words and sort them according to plural endings.
Children read aloud each list, listening for similar endings.

Individual work (ongoing for 1 or 2 days)

Children list other plural words from Chapter 1.
Children jot down any plurals from their current reading and writing.
Children add their words to the transparency list.

Whole class feedback (10 minutes)

Discuss what makes each list different.
Help the children to write some rules for making plurals:

> To make a plural, add *s*.
> When you hear an extra syllable, add *es*.
> When the singular word ends in a consonant then *y*, change the *y* to *ies*.
> (Continue, depending on the lists that the children have.)

Children write the appropriate rule at the head of each of their lists.

Assessment

Ask the children to write the plurals of words representing the different patterns that they found.

watch country cat peach baby elf

Grouping

The four-step spelling lesson is suitable for a whole class, for small groups, or for individual help. It is a good idea to make the small groups mixed-ability. A group of children all of whom have a limited vocabulary will not produce much worthwhile learning.

Benefits for the whole class

✔ Spelling patterns are the same for everyone. Whatever the children's level of vocabulary and language use, each will use the same patterns and concepts every time they write. The difference is in the words that they will use. Whole class learning becomes individual when children use the patterns that they have learned to enable them to construct the particular words they need for their own writing.

✔ In a large group, there are more children to contribute words and ideas. This will enable you to collect a useful number of words more quickly and move on to the next part of the activity.

✔ When you write down the children's words and ideas as they suggest them, you can collect information quickly. The "meat" of the lesson is not the list of words, but the discoveries that children will make from it.

✔ Working with the whole class does not single out poor spellers. Children can learn in a mixed-ability setting, and recognize that everyone needs to learn the same concepts.

✔ Non-native English speakers and children whose vocabularies are not large will have an opportunity to benefit from the words suggested by other children.

✔ You can demonstrate word-collecting and categorizing. With a little experience working with you, children will be able to work in small groups to do similar activities.

✔ You can take a few minutes at any time of the day and in any subject to pick out a subject-oriented word and make a list of related words. These might be *ology* words in science, *metre* words in mathematics, or *geo* words in geography. There will be many opportunities for a five-minute spelling lesson with the whole class.

Benefits for small groups

✔ Some children are more willing to contribute in small groups than in front of the whole class.

✔ Small groups can work physically with words, to cut them apart, sort and categorize them, discuss them.

✔ Whenever children work in small groups, talk is built into the process. Through negotiation, children can put forward their ideas, try out theories and justify their thinking. This will help them to think logically about spellings and see spelling as a problem-solving task.

Benefits for individuals

✔ When you are talking about spelling errors in a child's writing, you can focus on the specific words the child is using at the time they are needed.

✔ Work with individuals is private.

✔ As you work with individuals, you can assess each child's knowledge, attitudes, confidence and ways of thinking about words.

Teaching spelling through children's writing

Teaching opportunities

Writing provides not only the best motivation for spelling, but also the ideal place to practise building words. It also gives some excellent opportunities for teaching.

✔ When you talk with children about their writing, take some time to focus on words they are using.

✔ Make sure that you focus on spelling at the editing stage, rather than in the first flush of composition.

✔ Give children spellings that they need but which they have not yet learned. This will help them to keep the flow of their writing going and give them confidence to use more difficult vocabulary.

✔ When you give a spelling, point out one or two other words that fit the same pattern. Then ask the child to add more words. In this way, the child can place the new spelling in its own context and learn a spelling pattern.

✔ Make a note of patterns in the errors that children make. For example, they may add endings incorrectly, fail to use double letters or misspell a suffix. You can point out these kinds of errors and demonstrate how the child can correct them.

✔ Assess children's attitude towards spelling and writing. Are they confident or nervous? Do they take risks? Are they trying to use all the words in their speaking vocabulary, or do they stick to words that are easy to spell? Can they add words to a spelling pattern? Can they find their errors? Do they see themselves as good or as poor spellers? Does this affect their composition?

Drawbacks

While working through their own writing gives unique opportunities to help children on an individual basis, there are some drawbacks.

✔ Individual writing conferences and spelling conferences are very time-consuming. It is unlikely in a regular classroom that you will be able to give each child enough personal attention to consider this a major part of spelling instruction. Work with children on spellings in their own writing as much as possible, but supplement this with whole class and group instruction on a regular basis.

✔ Language is not a solitary activity. Working in groups with other children provides opportunities to engage in many word-collecting and word-building activities that children cannot do alone.

Responding to spelling errors

The way in which we respond to spelling errors will influence what the children feel is important, as well as their confidence and attitude towards spelling and writing.

In the past, teachers red-pencilled every error and returned the writing for the child to make corrections. More recently we have considered this to be discouraging for children and a negative influence on composition. This has often led to errors being ignored in favor of creativity. Neither of these approaches reflects an understanding of writing or of spelling. Rather than picking sides, we can take a more pragmatic approach.

We know that mistakes can lead to learning in every kind of endeavour, from cooking to carpentry. It would be ideal if this could also be the case in spelling. In order to bring this condition about, we must go back to the question of purpose. When and why do we mark spelling errors in children's writing?

There are three purposes for responding to errors:

✔ Editing function
✔ Instructional function
✔ Assessment function

As what we do is quite different in each case, it is vitally important that children know which of these is in effect.

Editing function

Editing is for the purpose of writing a final draft that has no errors, omissions or spelling mistakes. If we write a final draft that still has errors, it is not final and must be redone before going on public view.

In order to eliminate all spelling errors, writing must be proofread, every error located and the correct spelling substituted. If children see this kind of marking as a positive strategy, one that helps them at the next draft stage, they will be grateful for the help, not discouraged by the number of words you mark.

✔ When you have a piece of writing in front of you, whether the child is present or not, first consider the stage of the writing and what will happen to it next. If the child is preparing to write a final draft to be read by someone else, find and signal every error. Develop a code, perhaps underline the word, put an asterisk beside it, or write the correct spelling above.

✔ Establish yourself as a classroom editor, whose job it is to help to prepare manuscripts for final draft. Put up a sign, advertising your position, and listing what you will do to help.

PHENIX
EDITORIAL SERVICES

- Help with final-draft manuscript
- Spelling errors found
- Punctuation added
- Grammar tips free

YOU NEED IT... WE PROVIDE IT!

✔ Ensure that children see you making use of a range of dictionaries and reference sources as you edit. Make sure that the children have access to these materials as they proofread and that they use them to check their work. (See "Using a dictionary," p. 67.)

✔ Mark spellings with a color other than red. Red has pejorative overtones.

✔ Teach children to recognize and use some editing shortcuts and symbols, e.g., symbols for omissions, reversals or a new paragraph. These can make editing quick and easy.

✔ It is ideal if you can proofread and edit while the child is present. Then you can "talk through" the corrections you are making: "This is a question. What punctuation mark do you need?" "You have the *ie* the wrong way round here. Do you remember that rhyme for putting *i* before *e*?"

✔ If you edit when the child is not present, make sure it is clear that editing is what you are doing. Encourage children to ask when they need a final edit. They can write a note at the end of the writing: "Please help me to edit."

✔ Do not mark a large number of errors and ask the child to make all the corrections. If there are many spelling errors, the task is probably too great for the child to contemplate without discouragement. This will work against positive attitudes towards using a dictionary that you are trying to establish. Choose one or two words that you think the child can correct, suggest one or two to look up in a dictionary and indicate which these are.

✔ Establish the principle that children must do all the editing they can for themselves before asking for your help. You can set up a system of editing partners, so that each child can have someone to help with the proofreading. Children who are good spellers and good proofreaders can volunteer to have their names on an "Editing Partners" list, and help when they are asked.

✔ Children may be able to enlist editorial help at home, and ask for it only when they are preparing for a final draft. This will help families to understand when spellings need to be corrected and when they do not.

Instructional function

This kind of response is for the purpose of helping the child to learn something about spelling. For this, it is a waste of time trying to deal with a large number of errors. It is better to have real learning of one or two spelling concepts than to try for too much and have the child forget or be discouraged.

✔ Choose only one or two words for a spelling-instruction focus.

✔ When you focus on a word, give the correct spelling and help the child to fit it into its own spelling pattern. "This is how you spell *sock*. There is a *ck* at the end. It goes with *rock*. Can you think of another rhyming word?" In this way, you can help the child to learn a spelling pattern.

✔ Choose a misspelled word and help the child to think logically about the spelling. "*Mechanic* uses the same root as *machine*. That's why they both have *ch* inside. Can you add another word to this pattern?" In this way you can demonstrate the kind of reasoning that will help the child to work out spellings in the future.

✔ You can respond in these ways either verbally, as you talk to a child about the writing, or in writing, as you highlight a spelling error and comment on the child's page. If you respond in writing, invite the child to add more spellings to the pattern you have mentioned.

Assessment function

Deducting marks from a score because of spelling mistakes does not fit in with either of the above response functions and is not likely to help a child to become a better speller or writer. This does not mean that there is no place for making a judgment of a child's spelling. It does mean that you and the child must be quite clear about when assessment is taking place and what the criteria are.

✔ The most regular form of assessment will be for diagnostic purposes to determine what progress a child has made against his or her former attainment and what steps will be necessary to move him or her forward.

✔ Sometimes you will want to assess a child's spelling in relation to a norm for the child's age group.

✔ Sometimes you will be assessing the child's spelling according to the level you feel that child is capable of.

✔ Spelling and composition are totally different skills within the writing process. If you need to assign a numerical mark or a grade to writing, separate the different categories of writing skill and give the child a true value judgment for each one: composition, language usage, organizing information, spelling, handwriting. Spelling problems should not detract from a child's sense of achievement in other areas of writing.

✔ When you assess spelling in children's writing, be aware of whether it is first-draft writing, or whether the child has had an opportunity to proofread and edit. Assessment at all stages of writing is appropriate and useful, but will give you different kinds of information. In first-draft writing you will be able to see which words and patterns are automatic for the children. After editing, you will see which words and patterns the child can proofread for and correct.

✔ Use the assessment function sparingly. The prospect of assessment changes the character of a writing task. It discourages risk-taking and can lead to simple words and short sentences. The "what does the teacher expect me to write?" syndrome may take over and detract from the real purpose. The most revealing assessment takes place without the child's knowledge and is an ongoing record of concepts and skills that the child knows and is able to use in writing.

You can use all three methods of responding to spelling errors. If children understand the function of editing and final draft, they will not be confused when sometimes you focus on all the errors and sometimes you don't.

Make sure families also understand that you will sometimes mark all the spelling errors and sometimes ignore them. Children should be able to explain to their families why some writing has spellings corrected and some does not. If they cannot, it is a sign that the child does not understand the writing process.

Chapter 4

Teaching spelling patterns

Why teach spelling patterns?

Think of a spelling pattern as a group of words that share the same element of spelling for the same reason — sound, function or meaning. Spelling patterns are very useful when we are trying to work out the spelling of a new word. We need to teach children first that spelling is not random, but largely logical and highly predictable. Then we can help them to build up their knowledge of spelling patterns.

Perhaps the most important thing children can learn from studying spelling patterns is that knowing how to spell one word can help you to spell many other words. All you have to do is make the right connections. It is many-for-the-price-of-one learning.

Roots, prefixes and suffixes form the building blocks of words. We use them to build words just as young children use alphabet blocks to sound out words. Just like the alphabet blocks, word-parts can be taken apart and combined in different ways to make many different words.

Understanding word-parts and how to use them together is one of the most important skills of spelling. This knowledge will also help children to decode and understand new words that they meet in their reading.

A word of warning about spelling patterns

Sharing the same grouping of letters does not necessarily make words members of the same spelling pattern.

Although they share an ending that looks the same, these words do not belong to the same spelling pattern: *farmer, wiser*

This is a better way to group them:
   List *farmer* with *baker, potter, builder*   (the *er* ending denotes one who does a certain job).
   List *wiser* with *bigger, wetter, greater*   (the *er* denotes a comparative ending).

When you group words together for study, look for logical connections whenever possible. Try to answer the questions, "Why are these words spelled this way? What makes them similar?"

Four kinds of spelling patterns

There are four kinds of spelling patterns that can be helpful for children to learn about:

- ✔ Sound patterns
- ✔ Function patterns
- ✔ Meaning patterns
- ✔ Word-building patterns

Fitting a word into its "family," based on sound, function or meaning, can help children to make connections; the more connections they can make, the more predictable spelling becomes and the fewer spelling errors they will make.

Sound patterns

Sound patterns are those in which what we hear influences the letters we choose. For the beginning speller, this means listening to the sounds in each word and trying to match letters to the sounds; in other words, spelling by phonics. If we know the sounds represented by consonants, vowels and their various combinations, we can make reasonable predictions about how words are likely to be spelled.

Sound-pattern knowledge starts with phonics, as children learn about consonant sounds, consonant combinations, short- and long-vowel rhyming patterns, silent letters and so on. At first, children will over-generalize and use a pattern where it does not belong. They will learn a pattern but need to be told that there will be exceptions. (Some exceptions to recognizable patterns, such as *have, give, said, was*, are better treated as "sight vocabulary" and practised as separate items.) The more experience children have of reading and writing, and the more help in recognizing and building sound patterns, the more likely they are to choose the correct spelling. This process, however, is not automatic and even fluent readers need explicit teaching about spelling patterns both within and out of context. Children can build up their knowledge of sound patterns by collecting words that share the same sound and spelling.

Once they have learned a few basics about letter sounds, beginning writers spell almost entirely according to the sounds they hear, as these are the only patterns they have so far had a chance to learn. This is sometimes called "invented spelling" or "developmental spelling." Spelling phonetically gives children the opportunity to write using every word in their speaking vocabulary; they are not limited by their lack of spelling knowledge. As a result, the writing of young children is often as interesting and varied as their talk.

A beneficial side-effect of spelling-by-sound is that children become phonics experts and can apply this knowledge when they read. Phonics is far more useful and far more thoroughly learned and practised through spelling and writing than through reading.

Dialect note

As you work with sounds, be aware that vowel sounds are greatly affected by dialect. Words that rhyme in some dialects do not rhyme in others. In North American English, *ball* and *doll* rhyme. In the rest of the world, they do not. In the south of England, *bath* and *hearth* rhyme; in the north they do not. *Day* and *die* sound the same in several accents, including Australian.

Although vowel rhymes may vary from dialect to dialect, they remain constant within each person's speech. We can all build rhyming patterns that are meaningful for each one of us.

Strategies for teaching sound patterns

A study of sound patterns involves investigating the many ways in English in which we represent sounds with consonants and vowels. (For 99 ways to spell consonant sounds, 46 ways to spell short-vowel sounds, and 74 ways to spell long-vowel sounds, see *The Spelling Teacher's Book of Lists*.) This begins with basic letter sounds, or phonics, and progresses to ways in which these are combined to represent sounds.

✔ With beginning spellers, start with consonants, then move on to vowels. It is easier for children to hear and distinguish consonant sounds. Also, knowing a few consonant sounds will make it possible for children to start writing, and this is the purpose for it all.

✔ The best way to learn vowel sounds is by finding and building words with the same vowel rhyming pattern, and it is easier to do this if children already know some consonant sounds.

✔ Start with single letters, then progress to letter combinations.

✔ When you work with consonant combinations, ask children to listen for first one sound (*cat*), then two sounds together (*scat*), then three sounds together (*scrap*).

✔ The nasal *m* and *n* (*m* and *n* followed by a consonant: *jump*, *send*) are difficult for young children to hear. Do not try teaching these patterns to beginning spellers. There are many other sounds that are easier for them to learn at an early stage.

✔ Start with short vowels, then progress to long vowels. Most short-vowel sounds are made with one letter, while most long-vowel sounds need two letters. (Exceptions include the frequently used words *he, me, she, go, so,* as well as words ending in a final *o – tomato*.)

✔ It is not necessary to work through every letter and letter combination one at a time. Once children understand the principle of listening for letter sounds and combinations, they will work many of them out for themselves.

✔ Encourage children to write, whether they know enough letter sounds or not. They will be able to fill in more letters as they continue to learn more about sounds. Do not worry if you cannot read their spelling; the learning is not a result of our reading it, but in the child's continuing efforts to listen for sounds and match them with letters.

✔ Syllables represent one kind of sound pattern. While beginning spellers build words sound by sound, more experienced spellers build words syllable by syllable. Syllables often match up with prefixes, roots and suffixes, and being able to separate them can help to spell each part of a word correctly.

✔ It is not vital that children know how to divide syllables the way a dictionary does. It is helpful if they can identify how many syllables, or beats, there are, and build and proofread them one by one.

Raw materials for building sound patterns

Sound patterns are made with word-parts called "onsets" and "rimes." (Children need not know these terms.) Children can use onsets and rimes to build many words.

An onset (the beginning part of a word) may be a single consonant or a combination of two or three consonants.

These onsets each combine another letter with *l*:
> *bl, cl, fl, gl, pl, sl*

These onsets each combine another letter with *r*:
> *br, cr, dr, fr, gr, pr, tr*

These onsets each combine another letter with *s*:
> *sc, sk, sm, sn, sp, st*

These onsets each combine another letter with *w*:
> *sw, tw*

This onset sounds as if it is made with *w*, but it never is:
> *qu*

These onsets have two letters, but only one sound:
> *ch, ph, sh, th, wh*

These onsets have three sounds you can hear:
> *scr, spr, str, spl*

These onsets have three letters, but only two sounds you can hear:
> *shr, thr*

These rimes build words having a final, silent *e*:
> *ace, ade, age, ake, ale, ame, ate, ave*
> *eme, ese, eve*
> *ice, ide, ife, ike, ile, ime, ine, ipe, ise, ite, ive*
> *obe, ode, oke, ole, ome, one, ope, ose, ote, ove*
> *ube, ule, use, ute*

These rimes use vowel combinations:
> *aid, ail, ain, air*
> *ead, eal, eam, ean, ear, eat*
> *ie*
> *oar, oat, oe, oil, ood (wood), ook, oot (foot), ood (food), oof, oom, oon, oop, oot (shoot), ool, oor, owl, own, oy*
> *ue*

This is not a complete list of onsets and rimes. It illustrates the kinds of patterns that children will need to use in their writing.

For each sound that you investigate you can use the four-step spelling lesson described on p. 23.

This lesson focuses on the sound of *f*.

1. Collect words	2. Sort the words
List words with the sound *f* on an overhead projector. *safe, chief, phone, graph, elephant, laugh, tough, half, calf*	Give a copy of the list to children in small groups. The children are to cut apart the words, and sort them according to their spelling of the sound of *f*. *safe, chief* *laugh, tough* *elephant, phone, graph* *calf, half*
3. Investigate the patterns	4. Build more words
Bring the groups together to share and compare. Ask questions to help the children make discoveries about the words. How many patterns have you found? Which patterns have many words? Which have only a few words? Which spellings can come at the beginning of words? Which can never come at the beginning of words? Which vowel never follows *ph*?	Children use a dictionary and build a *ph* list for each vowel: A: *phantom, pharaoh, pharmacy, phase, phrase* E: *pheasant, phenomenon* I: *Philadelphia, philately, Philip, philosophy* O: *phobia, phonics, phony, phosphate* Y: *physics, physical*

Function patterns

Function refers to the way that a word is used in a sentence. Typically in English we add different endings to words to change their function. For example:

adjective	noun	adverb	verb
sad	*sadness*	*sadly*	*sadden*

Most suffixes are function patterns because they change singular to plural, verb tense or part of speech. The spelling of a suffix remains the same, no matter which word it is added to; if you can spell it in one word, you can spell it in all words. Knowing function endings can make spelling at least part of a word highly predictable.

Strategies for teaching function patterns

The best way for children to learn function patterns is to collect and build words that share the same function and ending. As they work with word endings, children will also gain an awareness of how words are used, and the different kinds of words that make up our grammar and syntax.

✔ Perform "function magic" to change the part of speech.
Add *y* to change a noun into an adjective:
funny, rainy, smelly, snowy
Add *ly* to change an adjective into an adverb:
wisely, swiftly, greatly, cunningly
Add *ment* to change a verb into a noun:
placement, adjustment, argument, judgment
Add *en* to change an adjective or noun into a verb:
widen, sharpen, lengthen, frighten

✔ Perform similar "function magic" to change a word's application.
Add *ist* to turn an object into a person:
harpist, typist, artist, balloonist
Add *y* to turn a person into a place:
pottery, bakery, grocery, fishery

✔ When the children are used to building words in this way, they can make endings "disappear" to change a part of speech. This will teach children to look for the different parts of words. Being able to recognize a prefix, root and suffix, and to separate them from one another, is very helpful in spelling.

✔ Collect different ways to make plurals. Most plurals are highly predictable; for example, the *s* ending that marks plural nouns is often pronounced like *z* (*dogs*) but is never spelled with *z*. It is a safe bet that, except for a few irregular plurals, *s* will be the final letter. Children will readily find examples of the three most common plural endings: *s, es, ies*. They may not so readily identify plurals such as *people, children* and *media*. Start a classroom list that the children can add to as they find more plural patterns. Although the vast majority of plurals that we use belong to the three regular patterns, there are a great many other plural patterns. Because these represent many different languages, they provide a good opportunity to teach the children about word origins.

dogs	*churches*	*babies*	*children*	*people*	*geese*	*mice*
sheep	*wolves*	*men*				

Latin:	*formulae*	*cacti*	*media*	*indices*
Greek:	*hypotheses*	*criteria*		
French:	*gateaux*			
Hebrew:	*cherubim*			

Children may be able to recognize some patterns-within-patterns in these plurals. For example, words with Latin origins tend to be used in science contexts, while words that do not change in the plural form are animals.

✔ In order to add endings to words correctly, children need to know the word-building patterns described below. To avoid the confusion of trying to teach more than one concept at a time, you can start off by giving children examples that do not require any change of the original word.

✔ Children will understand grammar more readily and be able to name parts of speech if they understand the functions of words. Looking at endings and how they change the way in which a word can be used will contribute to this understanding.

Meaning patterns

Dr. Johnson, author of the first great English dictionary, believed that English spelling owes more to meaning than to sound. This is why he maintained the different spellings of homophones; they may sound the same, but when you meet them in reading they look different.

"What is written without effort is in general read without pleasure."

The meaning of a word is often centred in its root, the spelling of which tends to remain the same even when a variety of prefixes and suffixes is added to it. Prefixes that alter meaning also maintain their spelling on all words, and do not change the words to which they are added.

Understanding a word's meaning and origin is helpful in spelling. If you know a word is medical, and that our science of medicine came from the Greeks, you will be able to predict that an *f* sound will be spelled with the Greek *ph* (*physician*). If you are writing about Italian food, you will know that many words end in *i* rather than the *y* your ear would lead you to expect (*fusilli*).

Children can build word-families of words that share the same root or prefix and learn how the meanings and the spelling remain constant.

Strategies for teaching meaning patterns

Meaning patterns involve roots and prefixes. When children understand the meaning of a root or prefix, they can use this knowledge to build words. Teach children to use meaning links to help them to spell words they are not sure of.

✔ Help children to understand that words are built up of different parts, each with its own meaning and function. With beginning spellers, start out with whole words to which prefixes and suffixes can be added.

farm er	*paint er*	*teach er*
free ly	*calm ly*	*foolish ly*
snow y	*smell y*	*munch y*
kind est	*cool est*	*hard est*
re use	*re model*	*re form*
un do	*un mask*	*un fasten*
pre cut	*pre form*	*pre mature*

✔ As you build lists of words that share the same root, children will come to expect the spelling of a root to remain the same in all the words. Point this out particularly in words in which pronunciation of the root changes, but the spelling does not.

please/pleasant   revise/revision

✔ Pay particular attention to prefixes that end with the first letter of the root to which they are added. These often cause one of the letters to be omitted.

mis spell, un natural

Children will avoid such misspellings if they know that all the letters of both prefix and root must still be included.

✔ Teach children to work out the spelling of new words by writing down one or two other words that may be connected in meaning. For example, listing *signature* and *signal* may help you to remember the silent *g* in *sign*.

LISTEN FOR THE SILENT LETTERS

Now You Hear it	Now You Don't
signal	sign
condemnation	condemn
muscular	muscle
columnist	column
autumnal	autumn
phlegmatic	phlegm
solemnity	solemn
agnostic	gnostic

✔ Compound words form a special kind of meaning pattern. Children need to know that all the letters of both words must still be present. This is particularly important when joining the two words results in repeating a letter in the middle (*bookkeeper, granddaughter*). In England, the compound word *granddad* has been misspelled as *grandad* for so long that this usage is now accepted as being correct.

✔ Many prefixes fall into meaning groups that are helpful for a teaching focus. Some larger dictionaries list these prefixes.

Numbers:	*uni, bi, kilo*
Size:	*micro, mega*
Where:	*circ, tele*
Negation:	*un, mis*
Opposites:	*pro/anti, bene/mal*

✔ Meaning is particularly important for spelling homophones. These are words that sound the same, but have different spellings and different meanings. In order to learn homophones, children must know the meaning of each word. It is more productive to teach each one in its own meaning context than to group them together into one lesson. These homophones do not form a spelling pattern: *there   their   they're*. Grouping them together is what makes them difficult to distinguish. It is better to put each word in its own pattern:

there	*their*	*they're*
thereabouts	*his*	*we're*
here	*her*	*you're*
where	*my*	*I'm*
everywhere	*our*	
therefore	*your*	
nowhere		
somewhere		

It is only by making the right meaning connection that children can choose the correct homophone spelling.

Word-building patterns

These are sometimes called "spelling rules," but this is a misnomer. There are no rules in English spelling, because there is no recognized authority to make them. Even the dictionaries reflect usage; they do not mandate it. Dictionaries recognize the evolutionary nature of spelling by listing alternative spellings that are in use in different dialects of English. However, there are some regular patterns in the ways in which we construct words, and knowing these can help children to make more correct choices about spellings.

The best way for children to learn one of these word-building patterns is to collect many examples and to look for the similarities. Once they make a generalization about a pattern, they can use it to construct other words.

Adding endings

There are four patterns for adding endings to words.

1. Double the final consonant

It is a common pattern in English that double consonants follow short-vowel syllables.

grabbed, messy, kitten, coffee, butter

When adding a suffix to a short-vowel syllable, double the final consonant.

can canned	*slip slipping*	*fun funny*

Children can learn this pattern by listing words using each vowel. You can also draw their attention to the change in meaning that a mistake can create:

canning or *caning?*	*pinning* or *pining?*	*ridding* or *riding?*

2. Change *y* to *i*

Some children find this confusing because it does not apply to all words ending in *y*. There are two ways to explain these patterns to them:

✔ When a word ends in a consonant + *y*, change *y* to *i*: *baby   babies*.
When a word ends in a vowel + *y*, just add the ending: *bay   bays*.
This is a linguistic definition and is sometimes hard for young children to understand and remember.

✔ When the last vowel sound that you hear is *y* all by itself, change *y* to *i*:
pon y   pon ies
When *y* is only part of the last vowel sound you hear, just add the ending:
mon key   mon keys

Whichever way you explain it, many children will find it confusing. The best way for children to internalize the pattern is to collect many words that illustrate the two ways of adding endings to words ending in *y*. Children can then both see and hear the difference. They will probably respond to the notion that it is important not to make the words look funny.

    ponys   *monkeies*

3. Drop the final *e*

We drop the final *e* because if we did not, some words would look very strange and "un-English." Show the children some examples of the kind of words we would make if we just added endings to these words:

    use + ed = useed   *rise + ing = riseing*   *wide + en = wideen*

These strange-looking spellings occur when two vowels come together. This is why we do not drop the final *e* when adding suffixes beginning with consonants; the problem just does not arise.

    safety   *useless*   *strangeness*   *vengeful*

If they see enough examples of both kinds of patterns, children will come to see their logic. When spelling is logical, children have a much better chance of remembering and using the patterns.

Recognizing when words look right and when they look strange is an important sense to develop. If children understand why to drop the *e*, it becomes a matter of common sense, rather than just another spelling rule that they have to remember.

4. Just add the endings

This one applies to all words in which one of the special cases described above does not apply.

i *before* e

There is a common rhyme we have all used to help to remember the order for these two vowels:

    i before *e*
    when it sounds like *e*
    except after *c*

It is important to remember that this pattern applies only to the long *e* sound.

 field   *believe*   *brief*
 receive   *deceit*   *ceiling*

Other vowel sounds will not follow the pattern.

 sleigh   *height*   *forfeit*

This makes it a series of relatively simple rhyming patterns, with few exceptions. Perhaps the most often misspelled of these is *seize*. (Names seem to be exceptions to this pattern: *Sheila, Reid, Keith, Neil, Madeira.* Any child with one of these names is likely to remember this pattern.)

Soft c and g

C and *g* are much influenced by the vowels that follow them in words. Here is a rhyme that will help to teach these patterns:

 I, y and *e*
 soften *c* and *g.*

This means that *c* or *g* followed by *i, y* or *e* will have a soft sound:

 civil   *cedar*   *cygnet*   *gender*   *ginger*   *gymnast*

C or *g* followed by *a* or *u* will have a hard sound:

 cat   *cup*   *gap*   *gust*

Children can take each pair of letters and build as many words as they can. Initially they will use the letters to start words, but older children can try to place the letters within the word.

 ca *ce* *ci* *co* *cu* *cy* *ga* *ge* *gi* *go* *gu* *gy*

Reading each list vertically will emphasize the sound caused by each vowel. It will also show up any exceptions that the children may find.

 Celtic *get*   *gills*   *tiger*   *girl*   *girder*   *girdle*

Knowing this pattern will also help children to see why they need to use *gu* for some hard *g* words:

 guest *guess* *Guernsey* *guild*   *guide*

spelling activities

Repertoire of activities

You will need a repertoire of activities for three kinds of spelling investigation:

✔ Word-collecting
✔ Word-building
✔ Pattern matching

You can then select an activity to suit each kind of spelling pattern that you are working with. The more variety in the activities, the more interesting spelling will be for the children and the greater the potential for learning.

Word-collecting activities

Spontaneous list

Use a starter-word or idea and ask the children to suggest words that fit the pattern. You can list the words as the children call them out, or ask them to work in small groups, each with a scribe. When you do this, children will often suggest a word that sounds as if it fits, but does not. You can list this to the side, explaining that it belongs in a different pattern that the children will learn about later.

Two ways to say ow

cow	brown	know	window
now	clown	blow	fellow
chow	drown	crow	below
how	howl	low	callow
allow	cowl	snow	tallow
scow	jowl	show	wallow
	fowl		follow
	scowl		tomorrow
	owl		sparrow
	prowl		
	down		
	town		

Some words can be pronounced both ways

bow	bow
sow	sow

Researched lists

When you introduce a word or pattern in class, you can ask children to look out for other examples as they read, write and go about their daily activities. They may go to specific sources, such as a dictionary, telephone directory or expert, to find words. Sometimes they may ask family members to help. When the children find a new word, they can add it to the list. After two or three days, or when there are enough words on the list, you can revisit it and help the children to learn about the patterns.

Example

If you are looking at words that end with a long *e* sound, ask the children to take along a notebook when they go to a supermarket, and write down food words that spell this final sound with *i*. Back in class, they can set this list beside a list of words that spell this final sound with *y*, then you can draw their attention to the fact that those ending in *i* are Italian.

Display

Set up a display of objects representing the same spelling pattern. You can start it off with one or two items, and ask the children to add other objects over the next day or two. Print a card to label each object as it is added. When the display is over, make the name cards available for children to sort, categorize, or put in alphabetical order. This is a basic skill needed for finding words in a dictionary.

Collages

Children can build letter collages by cutting out pictures of objects starting with the same letter. They can paste these on a large shape of the letter they are using. If children work in groups of three or four, the class can build a whole alphabet in a very short time. You can post these on the wall where the children can refer to them for letter sounds and shapes. Children will learn not only by finding pictures for their own collage, but also by identifying objects in the other pictures. Catalogues are good for cutting out pictures of objects.

You can extend this activity by asking the children to cut out words starting with the designated letter to make a word collage. They can build word collages for such groups as proper nouns, titles, different words meaning *street*, place names.

Rhymes

When you are working with a vowel pattern, children can often come up with a list of words by thinking of rhyming words. One way you can extend a list is by asking the children to try different consonants before and after the vowel sound in question. Use each consonant in turn through the alphabet and see what words it triggers.

Example

An alphabetical list of words rhyming with *air* might produce a list such as this:

> *air, bear, bare, care, dare, fair, fare, glare, hair, hare, lair, mare, pear, pair, pare, rare, share, spare, stair, tear, there, their, wear, ware, where*

When listed according to spelling pattern, it would look like this:

Words that rhyme with *air*

air	bear	bare	there	their
fair	pear	care	where	
hair	tear	dare		
lair	wear	fare		
pair		glare		
stair		hare		
		mare		
		pare		
		rare		
		share		
		spare		
		ware		

This will not only show children how many different patterns there are, but will help them to see which are the most common and which are rarely used.

Homework

Involve families in word collecting. After starting a collection in class, the children can ask their families to contribute other words. This is not only a way to increase the length and variety of your word lists, but also a good way to show families how their children are studying spelling.

Group themes

When children work in groups to collect words, give each group a different focus or theme. For example, if you are collecting adverbs ending in *ly*, groups could list words for ways to move in water, ways insects move, ways gymnasts move and so on. In this way, different groups are likely to come up with different words, and they can pool them to make a common list.

Observation post

Place the children in spots where they can observe action taking place, perhaps on the playground, in the gym, in the school office, at a street corner or on a family shopping trip. They can take a notepad, and list words in a particular category, perhaps adjectives ending in *y*, or past-tense verbs.

What are they doing?

In the gym	In the office	In the library	On the playground
jumping	typing	reading	throwing
vaulting	writing	viewing	shouting
climbing	talking	searching	playing
tumbling	sorting	asking	skipping
tossing	photocopying	whispering	batting

Personal dictionaries

Spelling instruction becomes personal when it helps the children with words that they need for their own writing. With a personal dictionary, children can keep words that they have trouble spelling, new words that they would like to use, words that they need for a particular task, and words that they find interesting. They can list family names, street names, birthdays and other words personal to their own lives. Children can select a few words that they think they might need from the word lists made in class and add them to their own dictionaries.

Beginning spellers who will be learning many new words might have an exercise book with a page for each letter. When they ask you for a spelling, you can print it on the correct page so they can find it again. Each time they add or look for a word, they will be practising finding information by using alphabetical order.

Theme words

When the children are working on a particular topic, it is often helpful to have a reference of words that they may need to use. These words are likely to be subject-related and can be difficult to spell. At the beginning of the theme, children can brainstorm a list of words that you can print on a chart to display for the duration of the study. Add any words you want the children to be able to use. As the theme progresses, you and they can add more words.

Children may be more willing to use difficult words if they are readily available. It is less time-consuming to find the words on a theme list than to look them up in a dictionary each time they are needed.

At the end of the theme, take the list down to make room for a new one. Keep the lists so they are accessible for the rest of the year. Store them on a chart stand, or list them to fit in a ring-binder. Before filing them away, ask one of the children to alphabetize the list.

Make sure the children do not see this list as words they have to memorize. It is not appropriate to test them on the words, except as they use them in their writing. You can, however, expect children to use the list when they are proofreading and editing their writing for a final draft.

You might use words from the list for spelling instruction by picking out one word at a time, and using it to build its own spelling pattern, to investigate its meaning and origin, and to build derivations (words built from a single root). If children continue to use some of the words in their writing, they may come to remember the spellings. If they do not continue to use them, they will be able to find them again in the future.

Word-building activities

Word wheels

This is ideal for building words based on the same prefix, root or suffix. Draw a wheel with the key word-part in the hub and different prefixes and suffixes in the outer rings. The children can list all the words they can make from the word-parts in the wheel.

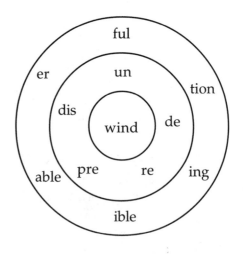

unwind
rewind
winding
winder

Word trees

A word tree is rather like a flowchart, and can grow branches or roots, or both (see p. 20). You can use a word tree to show derivations.

Letter cards

Beginning spellers can use cards with individual letters on them, then onsets and rimes to build words. Older children can use cards with roots, prefixes and suffixes on them to build longer words. Any time that children are manipulating letters to build words, they are learning about how letters work together.

If you keep a number of blank cards, children can add their own words and word-parts. They will enjoy making up their own games using the cards. As they make up the games, they will be finding ways to sort and to match the words.

Word frames

A word frame gives the beginning and end of a word, leaving the middle blank. Children can see how many different letters or letter combinations they can use to fill in the "picture." Beginning spellers may fill in one vowel between two consonants: *p__n, b__t.* Older children may fill in letter combinations: *m__ __l, p__ __t.*

You can reverse this activity by giving children the "picture" and asking them to frame it: *__ea__, __oa__.*

Extend the activity by not limiting the number of letters that children can use to make a word.

Child's list

_____ *ea* _____

beast	bread
bleat	breadth
bean	thread
creature	treasure
least	pleasant

Word webs

To start a word web, print a word in the centre of the board or a large piece of paper. You will want your web to branch off in more than one direction, so ideal words to start with are compound words, or words with a prefix or suffix. Take each part of the word in turn, and beside it list derivations. Then choose individual words from these new lists from which to build more derivations. Each list that you make will give you more words to start new lists. Word webs tend to go on forever, being limited only by the available space.

Word web

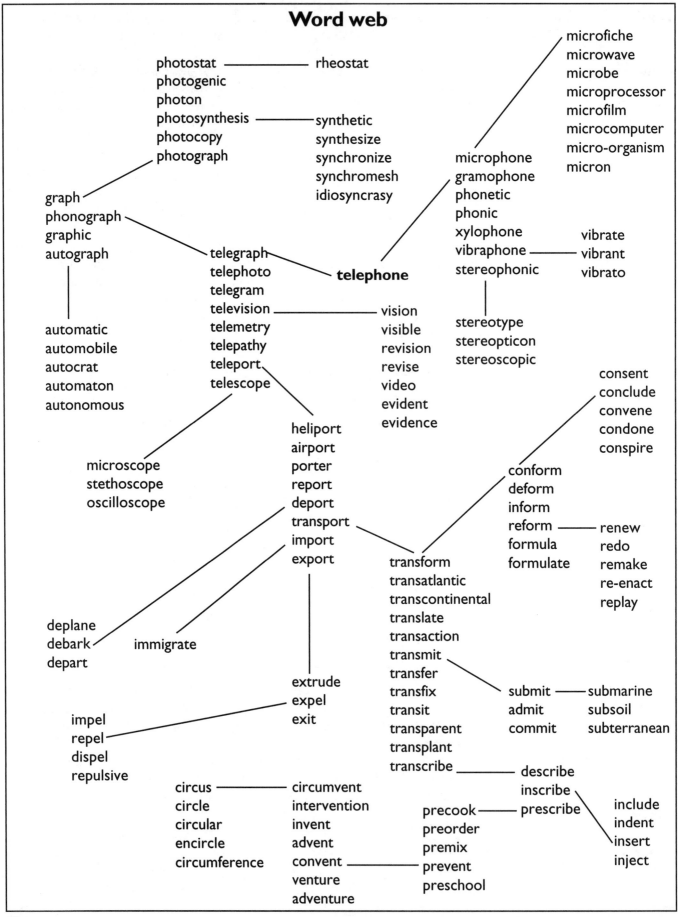

photostat —————— rheostat
photogenic
photon
photosynthesis ————— synthetic
photocopy   synthesize
photograph   synchronize
                             synchromesh
                             idiosyncrasy

microfiche
microwave
microbe
microprocessor
microfilm
microcomputer
micro-organism
micron

graph
phonograph
graphic
autograph

telegraph
telephoto
telegram
television ————— vision
telemetry   visible
telepathy   revision
teleport   revise
telescope   video
                   evident
                   evidence

telephone

microphone
gramophone
phonetic
phonic
xylophone
vibraphone ————— vibrant
stereophonic

vibrate
vibrant
vibrato

stereotype
stereopticon
stereoscopic

automatic
automobile
autocrat
automaton
autonomous

microscope
stethoscope
oscilloscope

heliport
airport
porter
report
deport
transport
import
export

consent
conclude
convene
condone
conspire

conform
deform
inform
reform ————— renew
formula   redo
formulate   remake
              re-enact
              replay

transform
transatlantic
transcontinental
translate
transaction
transmit
transfer
transfix
transit
transparent
transplant
transcribe ————— describe

deplane
debark
depart

immigrate

submit ————— submarine
admit   subsoil
commit   subterranean

extrude
expel
exit

impel
repel
dispel
repulsive

inscribe
prescribe

precook ————— prescribe
preorder
premix
prevent
preschool

include
indent
insert
inject

circus ————— circumvent
circle   intervention
circular   invent
encircle   advent
circumference convent ————— prevent
              venture
              adventure

Once children know how to build a web, they can work individually or in small groups to make their own. This is an ideal activity for children to do in groups, or to take for homework to involve the whole family.

Word searches

Finding words in a word search involves looking for letters that work in combination with one another. This will help children to distinguish between possible and impossible letter combinations. It can also help them to recognize theme words, high-frequency words or any words you want them to be able to read and use. You can introduce two levels of difficulty: provide the words, so the children have to find their match, *or* do not provide the words, and let the children discover them for themselves.

It is relatively easy to construct a word search. First make a list of the words you want to include. Take a grid of squares, and fill in a word across the top. Then try to fit in as many of your words as you can. Fill in the blanks with random letters. A well-constructed word search fills as many squares as possible with real words.

For young children, stick to words written horizontally. Do not expect them to find words written from right to left. For older children you can add words written vertically and, later still, diagonally.

Word mobiles

A mobile is one way to display words that are connected. After collecting words, the children can sort them into subcategories, and hang them from different strings on a wire coat-hanger. While most of the learning will be in finding the words and preparing the mobile, children will enjoy having their words on display.

Word chains

Build a word chain with a string of derivations. Start with a root, and add prefixes and suffixes one at a time to see how long it can grow. Print each word on a card and link the cards with paper clips.

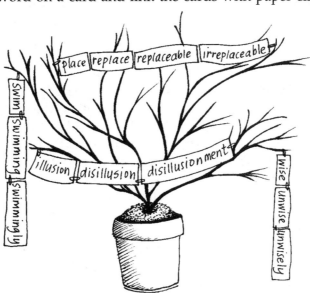

Word games

Give the children opportunities to play word games, such as crossword puzzles and Scrabble. Let them solve anagrams, and play Hangman. Any time children are building and manipulating words and letters, there is a potential for spelling learning.

Pattern-matching activities

Venn diagrams

Venn diagrams are ideal for sorting words, and sorting involves finding similarities among groups of words. For young children, start out with one circle, and ask them to put words that fit a pattern inside the circle, leaving the other words outside. Later, they can use multiple circles to sort words into different groups. When the children have learned how to sort using crossed circles in mathematics, they can apply this also to sorting words.

Concentration

Use any pairs of words to make a concentration game: upper and lower case letters, rhyming words, onsets, rimes, verb tenses, prefixes, suffixes and so on. The players place all the cards face down, and take turns to turn over two cards. If they make a match, they keep the cards and have another turn. When all the cards are picked up, the game is over.

Sorting

Cut apart words from a list, and ask the children to sort them in as many ways as they can. In order to do this, they will need to find ways in which the words are similar and ways in which they are different. This will help to teach them how to look for patterns and connections. They may sort according to rhyme, number of syllables, letter combinations, root, prefix, or suffix, or even such personal categories as words they use or do not use. After the sorting activity they should be able to explain and justify their choices either to you, to another child, or by labelling the categories. Children's justification for grouping words together is often the basis for a generalization that will allow them to use the same logic when trying to spell similar words in the future. This is the learning you want them to take away from a spelling lesson and is far more useful than a memory of the actual words.

Spelling investigations

Whenever possible, make spelling a "let's find out" kind of activity. You can use the four-step spelling lesson described on p. 23.

Ask a question, give a piece of information or form a hypothesis. Then:

1. Collect words.
2. Sort out the words.
3. Look for the pattern and logic.
4. Use the patterns to build more words.

When to use investigations

You can use these kinds of activities as the following:

✔ individual or group investigations
✔ homework assignments
✔ challenges for the whole family
✔ quiz-of-the-day on your bulletin board
✔ a follow-up to reading, using an example word from the text
✔ a starting-point for a spelling lesson
✔ activities for children who have misspelled similar patterns in their writing

Ideas for investigations

Here are some examples of the kind of questions you can ask to start such an investigation:

✔ In how many different ways can two vowels be combined? Write example words for each combination.

✔ In how many different ways can three vowels be combined? Write example words for each combination.

✔ Find words in which a long-vowel sound is made with only one letter. (Children should include *y* as one of the vowels that make a long sound. *Y* and *w* are considered vowels when they come at the end of a syllable but consonants when they begin a syllable.)

✔ Find words in which two vowels together make a short-vowel sound. (*head, forfeit*)

✔ What is the longest word you can write with only one vowel? (*Strengths* is probably the longest they will find. Attempting to build long words will involve trying out combinations of three consonants.)

✔ Find words that have *y* as their only vowel.

✔ Which vowel combinations can have more than one pronunciation? List examples of each. (*ea, ou, oo, oe*)

✔ The pattern *a_e* makes a long *a* sound. Which consonants can fill the space? Write words for each. (Repeat with each vowel.)

✔ *Ow* can have two pronunciations, as in *snow* and *cow*. Write examples for each sound. (Repeat for *ea* – *bread/bead* and *oo* – *foot/food*.)

✔ Which consonants can follow *s* in a word? Write example words for each combination. (Follow up with consonants that can follow *m*, or *n* at the end of a word.)

✔ Which consonants can come before *r*? Write example words for each combination. (Follow up with consonants that can follow *r* at the end of a word.)

✔ Which consonants can come before *l*? Write an example word for each combination. (Follow up with consonants that can follow *l* at the end of a word.)

✔ Which consonants can double at the end of words? Write three example words for each pair. Which are common? Which are rare?

✔ Are there any words that begin with a double consonant?

✔ Which consonants can pair with *h*? Write example words for each combination. Which can come at the beginning of words? Which can come at the end of words?

✔ Which is more common at the end of words: *c* or *ck*?

✔ Which letters can be silent at the beginning of words?

✔ List adjectives that end with a long *e* sound. How is this ending most often spelled? What other spellings are possible?

✔ What different suffixes can denote a person who does a certain job? (Start with examples, such as *act<u>or</u>, art<u>ist</u>, electri<u>cian</u>*.)

✔ Which words are spelled differently in American, Canadian and British English?

✔ Which words are spelled exactly the same as French words? (Extend the list by adding other languages.)

✔ What abbreviations can you find for titles and jobs? (Start with *Mr., Mrs., Dr.* The telephone directory will provide many more examples.)

✔ Which words can be abbreviated to form a contraction?

✔ In how many different ways can we make a word plural? (This is an excellent activity for children to take home. With the help of adults, they may find close to 20 ways.)

✔ Find words with four, five, or six syllables. What is the largest number of syllables you can write in a single word? (Finding a few words will involve a lot of syllable counting along the way.)

✔ The double letters found most often at the end of words are *ll, ss* and *ff*. Which vowels can come immediately before these endings? Write example words for each.

✔ When *ch* makes a hard *c* sound, the word is most likely of Greek origin. Write musical examples. Write scientific examples.

✔ Words ending in *eau* are of French origin. Write examples. Write the plurals of these words.

✔ When *ph* makes the sound of *f*, the word is probably of Greek origin. Find examples in which the *ph* comes at the beginning of the word, and examples in which the *ph* comes at the end of the word.

✔ The ending *ery* often denotes a place where a certain job is carried out. Write as many examples as you can.

✔ In compound words, all the letters of both words must be written. Write examples of compound words in which the last letter of the first word is the same as the first letter of the second word, as in *grand **d**aughter.*

✔ In consonant combinations in which both letter sounds are heard, the most common letters are *l, r* and *s*. Which consonants can combine with these? Write example words for each.

✔ *Ology* is a Greek suffix meaning the *science of* or *study of*. Write as many *ology* words as you can. Illustrate/mime/explain the meaning of each. Turn each one into a person by changing the suffix to *ist*.

Chapter

6

Using spelling lists

Using lists of words

Lists of words have always played a part in spelling instruction. Typically, children have spent a week memorizing a list to prepare for a test. Activities have been designed to allow the children to read and write the words many times, in the hope that this would imprint the word indelibly on their memories. Most teachers have seen children spell words correctly on the test, then misspell them in their own writing. Many children failed every week to get all their words right.

Lists of words play an important part in spelling learning. However, they should be lists that illustrate spelling patterns, not lists to memorize. When we understand the logical nature of spelling, we can use lists of words more effectively to help children to learn to spell.

Children can make use of three kinds of lists:

- ✔ Word family lists
- ✔ Reference lists
- ✔ Prompt lists

Word family lists

The hardest and most short-lived way to learn a spelling is to try to remember a word in isolation. As most words fit into spelling patterns, learning to spell one word can contribute to our learning of all the other words in the same pattern.

A word family list is designed to help children to recognize the similarities among words. Then when they want to spell a new word, they can try to match it to other similar words.

Spelling instruction is most effective when we can help children to think of words in "families," words that share the same spelling pattern. A large part of the learning takes place in the construction of the list, as children recognize the pattern and find words that fit. It is not necessary for children to try to memorize all the words. All they need to remember is the pattern; they can then reconstruct the words when they need them, as well as make reasonable predictions about the spelling of new words as they learn them.

Suggestions for word family lists

Any two or more words that have some connection with one another can form a word family. Your lists will represent three kinds of spelling patterns. The following is not a complete list of spelling patterns; it represents the kind of patterns children need to use in their writing.

Sound patterns

Consonants	Single	*b, d, f, g*
	Double	*bb, cc, dd, ff*
	Combinations of 2	*br, cr, dr, fr, sc, sk, sl* (two sounds)
		sh, th, ch, ph, gh (one sound)
		th, sh, ph, gh (new sound)
	Combinations of 3	*spr, str* (three sounds)
		thr, chr, shr (two sounds)
		tch, ght (one sound)
Vowels	Short	*a, e, i, o, u*
	Long	silent *e*, *igh(t)*
	Double	*ee, oo*
	Combinations	*ai, ea, ie, oa, ui*
	r controlled	*eer, ear, or, are*
	l controlled	*eel, eal, ail*
	Diphthongs	*oi, ow, oy*
Silent letters	Beginning	*kn, gn, pn, ps, mn*
	End	*lf, lm*

Function patterns

Verb tense	Regular	*d, ed, ing*
	Irregular	*was, flew, meant*
Plurals	Common	*s, es, ies*
	Foreign origin	Latin, Greek, French
	Rare	*en, ice, ren*
Suffixes	Derivations	*tion, ly, ful, ness, ment, able*
	How to add	plain, drop final *e*
		double final letter, change *y* to *i*
Contractions	Words contracted	*not, will, am, are, is, has, have, us*
Abbreviations	Titles	*Mr., Mrs., Dr.*
	Addresses	*St., Ave., Blvd., Cres., Dr., Rd.*
	Days	*Mon., Tues., Wed.*
	Months	*Jan., Feb., Mar.*
	Measurements	*m, km, ft, in, kg, l*
	Acronyms	*RADAR, SONAR, SCUBA*
	Words	*Fax, mini, phone*
Punctuation	End	period, exclamation, question
	Medial	comma, quotation
	Possessives	*'s, s'*
Capitalization	Proper nouns	people, places
	Sentences	

Meaning patterns

Compound words	Building All letters of both words	snow, ball, light granddaughter, withhold, bookkeeper
Roots	Latin Greek	port, sign, dict, fact, flect, ject, circ, cap, script, urb graph, geo, photo, therm, hyd, mech, scop, chem, aero
Prefixes	Negation Number Size When Where Again Judgment Latin Greek	un, dis, mis, in, im, il, non uni, bi, tri, milli, dec, kilo, multi micro, mega, mini, maxi pre, post, ante sub, super, tele, in, ex, trans, mid re pro, anti, con, contra mono, pre, aqua phono, psych, phys, cycl, therm
Sight words	Commonly used Pronouns Theme words	the, because, they, who my, his, her, our, their

Here is an illustration of a silent letter family:

The silent *h* family

whack	wheat	which	whisk	whoa	why
whale	wheedle	whichever	whisker	whorl	
wham	wheel	whiff	whisper		
wharf	whelk	while	whist		
what	whelp	whilst	whistle		
whatever	when	whim	Whitby		
	whenever	whimper	white		
	where	whimsical	whither		
	whereabouts	whinny	whiting		
	wherry	whip	whittle		
	whet	whippet	whiz		
	whether	whirl			
	whey				

Reference lists

A reference list takes the place of a dictionary. It is intended for temporary use, to give children words they need for a particular topic or project. Looking up words on a list takes less time than using a dictionary, yet can get children used to using such a reference to find out about words. A reference list is particularly useful in content-area subjects, where specialized and technical vocabulary may be too difficult for children to learn.

You can build such a list by first asking the children to brainstorm words that they think they might need for the topic. They can do this as a class while you record the words, or they can work in small groups first listing the words, then exchanging with another group for proofreading and finally checking the spellings with a dictionary or spellchecker. As the theme progresses, you or the children can add new words as you meet them in reading, or need them for writing.

Encourage children to list their words in alphabetical order, then each time they use the list they are practising the skills they need for using dictionaries and other reference books. If children build their own lists, they will learn the value of correct spelling, accurate copying and neat handwriting.

A reference list can be quite long, as its function is to be a mini-dictionary. When the theme is over, the list could be stored either in a file box or a ring-binder to be consulted when children write about this theme in the future. Children would then be able to refer to these lists during independent research or writing. A useful strategy is to select a certain number of these words for groups of children to rewrite as a glossary to be kept at the back of a file containing information on particular topics or subjects.

Children can use the word lists when they are writing or editing. You can make them responsible for proofreading for list words before their writing goes to final draft. Proofreading is generally more successful when children know what they are looking for.

Revisiting words from lists

Make sure that children do not see the reference list as a list of words to be memorized by rote. Using words frequently in context is the best way to learn new spellings and vocabulary. If children continue to use some of the words after the theme is over, they will more likely remember the spellings. You will find that frequency of use will help the words to pass into children's speaking and writing vocabularies.

Take every opportunity to revisit the words and use them in the classroom, even when the theme is over.

✔ Point out a list word when you meet it in a reading activity.
✔ Draw the children's attention to a list word in the news, for example a newspaper article about space exploration could allow you to revisit space words.
✔ Help children to understand and internalize new vocabulary by using it in class discussion and general conversation.

✔ Have a word-of-the-day. Print a word from a previous list on the board and encourage children to use it in speech and in writing.

✔ When the theme or project is over, you might give a short dictation to discover which words have become part of the children's sight vocabulary.

Word-play activities

In addition to using their words for writing, children can also use them in word-play activities such as the following:

✔ Print each word on a card. The children can alphabetize the cards to the first, second or subsequent letters.

✔ Take a closer look at some of the individual words. You might investigate a Latin or Greek root, or explore a word's origins.

✔ The children can sort the words in a variety of ways: meaning connections, number of syllables, prefixes, suffixes, parts of speech, or any category that they can devise for themselves.

✔ Use the words to build an illustrated alphabet book. This could also double as a glossary to help children to learn new vocabulary.

✔ Make a collage of the words. The children can use fancy script to print each word, or experiment with fonts from a computer.

✔ The children can test each other informally and in private to find out which of the list words they know already. They could then make shorter, personal lists of words that they cannot spell and need as a reference.

✔ The children can devise spelling tests for their families. Each child can choose what he or she thinks are the most difficult words on the list, and take them home to administer the test. In doing this, children will be raising their own awareness of words with which they have the most trouble, and will be rereading and checking them. It can also give you insights into which words children find difficult.

✔ The children can use list words to make a chant or rap. Pay attention to syllable count, and arrange the words to fit a particular rhythm. For example:

> Countdown, blast-off, galaxy, moon.
> Meteor, telescope, satellite, sun.

Several small groups can each develop a chant, then repeat them in turn while the whole group claps the rhythm. You can even sing them to an appropriate tune such as "Twinkle, twinkle, little star."

Prompt lists

A prompt list is for learning new spellings that do not fit a pattern that the children know.

Children all learned to spell their own names through frequency of use. They managed it because learning it was important to them, and because they saw and wrote their name many times. The best way to learn words in which the spelling is not predictable is through frequency of use, both in reading and in writing.

Frequency of use is only helpful if the children spell the words correctly each time they write them; otherwise, they may just become accustomed to using a misspelling.

Young writers need many "sight" words as soon as they begin to write. Service words, like *the, said, why, because,* are hard to sound out correctly, and belong to patterns that the children will not learn until much later. Older children will also need to learn some words by sight, either because they belong to no recognizable pattern, or because they are exceptions to familiar patterns, or because the children have not yet learned enough about words to recognize the patterns.

Hints on prompt lists Trying to memorize these words in isolation on a list is not effective; they may pass into short-term memory long enough for children to pass a test, but if they are not used regularly, many children will soon forget them. However, children can print a few at a time on a reference list and have it beside them when they write or edit.

✔ List high-frequency words that the children need but have not yet learned. You can make common lists for beginning writers, containing the most frequently used words. As children learn words at different rates, the lists will soon become more individual.

✔ Children can make their own lists of words that they misspell frequently in their writing. They can add new words as they discover them in their writing, and delete those they no longer need.

✔ Keep the list short, perhaps five words at a time.

✔ When children need one of the words in their writing, they should look for it on their list and write it correctly; when they become more confident, they can try to write it then check the spelling with the list afterwards.

✔ Make children responsible for checking their prompt-list words every time they write; they will only learn the spellings if they write them correctly. Looking for specific words is also the best way to learn the skill of proofreading.

✔ As children find they can write a word correctly without looking on the list first, they can cross it off. Every crossed-out word is a visible sign of learning. When all the words are no longer needed, children can have another group of words to use and learn.

Core vocabulary lists

Many schools have a list of words that children are expected to be able to spell by a certain age. They are usually high-frequency words that the children will need in their daily writing, or words that are frequently misspelled. As these come in lists, perhaps one for each year of school, it is tempting to slip back into old ways of expecting children to memorize the list.

How to use these lists

Listing words together does not make them into a spelling pattern. Unrelated words cannot effectively be learned as a group. Regard these lists as guidelines for planning the content of your spelling curriculum. Then children can learn these words in the same way that they are learning all the other words they need.

✔ Place each word in the list in its own spelling context, and teach it in the same way that you are teaching all the other words the children are studying.

✔ Look for the significant features of a word; what makes it predictable and what could make it difficult to spell. It is usually possible to predict the kind of error that children will make, perhaps omitting a silent letter, or incorrectly adding an ending. This will help you to find a suitable context for teaching the word.

✔ Use the list as an assessment checklist for each child. Note whether the children can spell the words in their daily writing.

✔ For those words that do not seem to fit with any others, put a few of them at a time on a prompt list, so the children can keep them handy when they write. After looking them up on the list a number of times, and using them regularly, the children may spontaneously remember them. Frequency of use in writing is one of the best ways to learn this kind of word.

✔ Make children responsible for words they have studied or that they have on their personal prompt lists. They can keep their own checklists to show which of the words they know and can proofread for.

Look, say, cover, write, check

By their very nature, the high-frequency vocabulary words will need to be used almost every day in children's writing. Many will be covered through the same patterning approaches already discussed. Through regular practice, children will learn even those that may seem to be exceptions to rules or follow no predictable pattern. One means of helping children to hold these words in their short-term memory is to use a "look, say, cover, write, check" method. This method has many variants. Although many classrooms will declare that they use it, it can become little more than a mantra for children if not properly taught. One child in a Lancashire, England daycare knew it as the "look, cover, write, cheat" method!

Look

✔ Look carefully for patterns, analogies with known words and any "tricky" conventions.
✔ Try to "hold" the word in the mind.

✔ If the word has syllables, break it up into parts and try each part before attempting the whole word.

✔ Look particularly for vowel combinations.

Say

✔ Vocalize each syllable.

✔ Sound the beginning and final sounds; remember particularly any silent or unvoiced sounds.

✔ Say the sounds and word again as you write it; this helps to fix it in the mind.

✔ If the word is practised on a separate notepad or in word-book, it is particularly important to "say it again" as it is written into the piece of writing.

(Some children, especially those with dyslexia (one of many learning disabilities), find it easier to *name* letters than to use their sounds when spelling.)

Cover

✔ This is particularly important as it helps to transfer the word into the memory.

✔ Some children need training to "hold" a picture in their imagination. Train them using a TV screen in their heads that they must switch on and picture a topical advertisement containing letters or words, e.g., cereal ads, hamburger restaurants and designer fashions.

✔ It sometimes helps if they visualize the words in color.

✔ Ask children to find words at a word table, and then hold them in their heads until they get back to their own seats.

Write

✔ This is where mistakes are often made in copying. If necessary, break the word up into sensible units or syllables.

✔ Copying from a classroom black/white board is particularly hazardous for many children who have to look up and down again constantly. If possible, provide them with a photocopied sheet of any large amounts of copied text so that they can place it nearer to themselves.

✔ Write, if possible, in cursive writing; this helps the children to "feel" the correct movements.

✔ It is even better if the children write *with their eyes closed* to place the emphasis on feeling; we often "feel" that we have misspelled a word before we see the error. If we can write a word with our eyes closed, it has become "automatically" learned. Practising this again to make absolutely sure is called "overlearning."

Check

✔ It is always easier to check someone else's work. Encourage children to check each other's practice words as well as proofreading their writing.

✔ Hold lessons in proofreading skills at each stage; as children progress as writers, the practice in this helps them to become more skilled at spotting errors including their own.

✔ Appoint a group, including less-able spellers, as "Official Spellcheckers" for a day and provide them with a range of references. Encourage the other children to take their work to this group to be checked. This could become a standard *independent* activity when writing is in progress.

Strategies for specific words	Regard each of the words as the subject of its own spelling investigation, along with other words that share a pattern. Here are some examples:
A lot	The mistake people make is to write *alot*. (My spellchecker corrects this to *allot*.) Teach this with *a little*, which no one would ever want to write as one word. Teach children to say *a little* whenever they want to write *a lot*. Sing the song, "Little Things Mean a Lot." You never know what kind of trigger will help children to remember spellings.
Their	Put this word in a list with other personal possessive pronouns: *my, our, his, her*. Then give children plenty of practice using these pronouns in sentences. They must understand the meaning in order to choose the correct homophone. It might help to point out that *he* and *I* are both in this word, and *her* is not hard to find. Never link it with *there* or *they're*; this will only add confusion.
Every	Children may omit the central *e*, as they do not pronounce it. Link this with compound words using *ever: evergreen, everlasting, forever*. The children can then build a pattern using *every: everyone, everywhere, everyday*.
They're	Teach this along with other contractions. Recognizing that this is really two words is essential to choosing the correct homophone spelling. Children will often misspell this word in first-draft writing. See if they are able to find and correct it when they proofread.
Too/Two	*Too* is one of the most misspelled words throughout school. Like most homophones, the word itself is not difficult to spell. The mistake is in choosing the wrong spelling, or in not being aware that there are alternatives. Children will often write *to*, no matter which homophone they need. Always teach *two* along with the other words related to the number *two: twins, twice, twelve, twenty*. The story of the Three Bears is ideal for teaching *too: too hot, too cold, too hard*, and so on. Exaggerate the sound; encourage children to write *tooooooo*, adding as many *o*s as they like. Tell them that *too* has too many *o*s. Do anything that will draw attention to what makes this word different from *to*. One of the keys to teaching homophones is to make children aware of them, so they stop and think which one to write and can proofread for them.
Tomorrow	Children often put *mm* instead of, or as well as, *rr*. Teach them that this used to be two words: *to* and *morrow*. *Morrow* was a noun, as in *"on the morrow."* If children think of *morrow* as a separate word, and write it as such, they are unlikely to prefix it with *tom*. The more children understand about a word's meanings and origins, the more likely they are to spell it correctly.
Because	This word is also best learned by looking at its history. It is a short form for *be the cause*. When they say *cause*, children are more likely to be guided by the pronunciation and less inclined to write *becos*.
Before	The challenge here is to get children to add the final *e*. Teach them the meaning of *in front of* or *ahead of*, and build this spelling pattern of compounds: *forehead, forecast, foreground, forefront, foremost, foremast*. Children can ask at home to find out the meaning and significance of shouting *"fore!"* It might come in handy in the classroom or playground.

Once

Link this with other words with a connection to *one*:

one	lone	unit
once	lonely	unify
only	lonesome	unicorn
	alone	uniform

Children can use the mnemonic *only once*. (A mnemonic is a memory trigger. The word comes from Mnemosyne, the Greek goddess of memory and mother of the Muses. Older children will enjoy linking this with *amnesia*, in which they will be able to hear the silent *m*.) Reading and writing the word in stories starting "Once upon a time ..." is also a good way to encourage children to use the word frequently.

Knew

Children can first learn about the silent *k* by building a word tree or word wheel with these words: *know, knowledge, knowing, knowledgeable, unknown*. They can then link *knew* with this past-tense pattern: *know/knew; blow/blew; grow/grew*. Children can then have some fun by noting that *flow* and *flew* are not part of the same verb. Perhaps they can find more silly examples, like *crow* and *crew*. Noting the anomalies of spelling and playing with words adds interest and can also lead to learning.

Which

This fits with a group of question words, all starting with *wh*. They are listed nicely in the Kipling poem:

I keep six honest serving men.
They taught me all I knew.
Their names are Who and What and Why
And When and Where and Who.

This is a good list of question words for children to keep beside them when they are doing research or conducting an interview. It could form a specialized prompt list for the classroom wall.

Sure/Sugar

Sure and *sugar* are the only words in which an initial *s* is pronounced like *sh*. They form their own spelling pattern, along with derivatives like *surely, ensure* and *sugary*. Put the words on the board for a few days. Children can challenge their families to think of words in which an initial *s* sounds like *sh*. This will give children a chance to be the spelling experts at home. To give them practice in using the words, they could use a dictionary to find compounds and phrases using *sure* and *sugar: sugar beet, sugar cane, sugar-coated, sugar loaf, sugar maple; surefire, sure-footed, for sure, sure enough, make sure*.

Enough	This belongs in two spelling patterns. Children can collect words in which *gh* sounds like *f*. If they know about words in which *ph* sounds like *f*, they will note that while *ph* can come at the beginning or at the end of a word, no word or even syllable starts with *gh*. They can also collect words that have the letter string *ough*, and list them according to their different pronunciations: *enough, tough, rough; cough, trough; bough, slough; dough, doughnut.*
Really	This word also can be looked at in two patterns. First, the *real* pattern: *realistic, realism, unreal, reality.* In many of these words, children will be able to hear both vowels and know with certainty what they are. It can also form part of a look at how to add the adverb ending *ly: nicely, quickly, wisely, coolly.* The usual patterns for adding endings apply: add the *ly* to the whole word, drop a final *e*, change *y* to *i*. An offshoot of this pattern is words ending in *ic*, to which we add *ally: electrically, politically.* Follow this up by looking at words ending in *ic* or *ick* and see if the children can work out what makes the two groups different. One spelling investigation often leads to another. Be prepared to be spontaneous and follow up any interesting or puzzling phenomena.
Girl/First/Birthday	Children often reverse letters to write *gril*. A vowel + *r* combination is difficult to sound out and can produce reversal errors in words like *park* and *first*. Beginning spellers often omit the vowel completely and need to learn that every syllable must have a vowel. Group together words with this "*r* controlled vowel" to form rhyming patterns. Find words ending in *ar, er, ir, or, ur*, and ask the children to add other letters at the end to make new words: *fir – firm, for – form, fir – first.*
Opened/Called/ Turned/Walked/ Followed	Look for words with similar prefixes, roots or suffixes, and group them together. These all belong in a past-tense verb pattern. Looking at past tenses will also generate a list of irregular past tenses that you can put on a reference list for the classroom.
Messy/Swimming	Many errors are caused by an inability to add endings to words correctly. Group these together and ask the children to categorize them according to the four ways to add endings (see pp. 39–40).
They're/Don't/Didn't	Group contractions together and make sure the children can read them correctly. Practice in writing the complete words along with their contractions may reinforce this pattern.
Together	Children will be interested in seeing the three little words that make up this word. Often finding a word interesting is enough to help them to remember the spelling.
Children	Once children know how to spell the sound of *ch*, this is not a difficult word. Until they learn it, they can put it on a prompt list.

Getting spelling right

Demonstrating strategies

Children often link poor spelling with lack of intelligence. They can also see adults as being infallible.

It is extremely important for children to see their teachers using the same strategies as they do. Putting some "deliberate mistakes" on a board or flip-chart can help to train them to spot errors.

Many teachers keep a dictionary handy on their desks to demonstrate the need for all of us to refer to particular words to check our spelling. It may take longer in the initial stages to help children to find a word that they wish to spell rather than writing it out for them, but in the longer term it helps them to develop independent strategies.

When does spelling count?

Children often ask this question when they are asked to write. Children need to know when they should have their spellings correct and when spelling should not be a primary focus of attention. When writing is to be read by another person, correct spelling is far more important than if the writing is for the writer's eyes only. Even when writing is for a public audience, a focus on spelling belongs at the editing stage, not during the composition of the first draft.

There are two questions any writer must ask before embarking on a piece of writing:

✔ What is it for?
✔ Who is it for?

Whether we are writing a shopping list or a party invitation, a story or a business letter, answering these two questions will let us know exactly what the task entails. The importance of spelling is directly linked to purpose and audience. The more we want to make a good impression, the more trouble we take with spelling and neatness.

If children focus on spelling at appropriate times in the writing process, they will be able to give it their undivided attention at the editing stage.

Strategies to link to the writing process

✔ Make sure that every writing activity in the classroom reinforces the writing process.

✔ Provide many opportunities for children to write for audiences both inside and outside the classroom.

Proofreading

Proofreading is not an innate ability; it is a learned skill. It is quite different from reading a story or finding a name in a telephone book. Children need instruction in how to go about it and regular practice in proofreading their own and other people's writing. It is not enough to say, "Read through your writing and see if you can find any spelling mistakes." Many children, and adults, do not find their errors, even when they know how to spell the words.

When we teach children to read, we try as soon as possible to stop them finger-pointing and reading word by word, and instead teach them to absorb larger chunks of meaning. Fluent reading demands that the reader predicts what will come next and only looks at enough of the text to confirm these predictions. Most of the time we actually decode only parts of words and often skip over words completely. This is a strength in reading, as it increases speed and understanding. However, this kind of reading is not productive for proofreading.

Proofreading is not a skill of looking "at"; it is more a skill of looking "for." If we know what we are looking for, we are much more likely to find it. Create and give children proofreading checklists of what to look for.

Strategies for teaching proofreading

✔ When children have had little experience, ask them to proofread for one concept only: capital letters at the beginning of sentences; quotation marks when someone is talking on the page; two or three high-frequency words.

✔ Encourage children to point to each word as they proofread. This will slow down the reading and remind them to look at every word. It can also be helpful to move a finger or pencil down the left-hand margin, or move a ruler down line by line.

✔ Put a symbol in the margin against lines with a spelling error. Then ask the child to find the mistakes in those lines. You need not always mark every error; limit the task to the words and the amount you feel the child has the experience and knowledge to handle.

✔ Point to misspelled words and ask the child to find the error. "You have left a letter out of this word. Can you put it back in?"

✔ Children can make their own lists of words that they have trouble spelling. They can use this as a reference for proofreading.

✔ Children can work together to proofread for each other. It is often easier to find someone else's mistakes, as you do not get so caught up in the meaning.

✔ Encourage children to proofread several times, looking for different kinds of errors each time. One read-through can be for punctuation, another for specific words, another for capital letters, and so on. Even professional proofreaders do not expect to find all the errors in one reading.

✔ Reading aloud is often helpful. When children stumble over the meaning, it can be a signal that something is wrong with the sentence, perhaps an omitted word or punctuation mark. When children cannot see that words have been omitted, it can be helpful for someone else to read their writing aloud to them.

✔ Help children to see words in their component parts: onsets, rimes, syllables, prefix, root, suffix. This can help them to proofread each part to make sure the spelling is correct.

✔ It is still important to read for meaning while proofreading. You cannot tell if a verb has the wrong ending, or if subject and verb do not agree, or if the punctuation is wrong, if you read each word as a separate entity.

✔ You can only expect children to proofread for words and spelling patterns they know. Make sure they get all the help they need to find and correct words they have not yet had a chance to learn.

✔ Remember that extensive proofreading is only purposeful when it is in preparation for a final draft. Laborious correcting can discourage children from writing. Little and often is a good rule for teaching the skill of proofreading.

✔ Sometimes children think that being a good writer means getting everything right the first time around. If they hold this belief, they may regard errors as a sign of weakness or inadequacy. Ask someone at your local newspaper or a publishing company to provide marked-up copy for the children to look at. Show them that everyone needs to proofread and make corrections, even the professionals.

Using a dictionary

For many children, a dictionary is not a friendly object. This may be because they cannot find the information they need quickly enough. It may be because looking up all their spelling mistakes takes too long and distracts them from more interesting aspects of writing.

A dictionary is such a basic tool for a writer that it is worth taking time to help children to make friends with their dictionary.

Strategies for teaching dictionary skills

✔ The basic dictionary skill is using alphabetical order. Anything that makes children familiar with using the alphabet is a dictionary skill. Alphabetize anything you can in the classroom: coat hooks, books, storage boxes, art equipment. The more often children find things using alphabetical order, the more it will become automatic for them.

✔ Teach children to distinguish among the different kinds of information in a dictionary: word, origin, derivations, definitions, examples. Sorting out the relevant piece of information and ignoring the rest is one of the skills of using a dictionary.

✔ Many dictionaries have more information than is necessary for spelling. When all you need is to find a spelling quickly, definitions, origins, examples and grammar tips get in the way and slow down the task. Direct the children to a Spelling Dictionary when all they need is to check a word.

✔ Keep a large-print dictionary, even for older children. Anything that makes finding a word quick and easy is helpful.

✔ Try to have a dictionary for each child. Then you can play dictionary games and give children daily practice in finding words.

✔ Any reference book that uses alphabetical order will teach children how to use a dictionary. Copies of your local Yellow Pages are often available free at the end of the year and will give you a resource for search games and puzzles. If you take two or three minutes a day and ask the children to find one or two pieces of information, dictionary searching will become a game and children will learn to find their way around a reference book quickly and easily.

✔ Gear the time children spend looking up their errors in a dictionary to the total time they spend writing. Using a dictionary should be a regular task, but should not become an overwhelming part of writing time.

✔ Be alert for the children who overuse a dictionary. If they try to look up too many words during the course of first-draft writing, they will find composition next to impossible. Encourage children to place a mark beside words they are not sure of, and to check them at the end of the writing time, or when the first draft is finished. A child who will not write without having all the correct spellings first is not a risk-taker. Direct this child to the try-it! strategy (see p. 17), and offer proofreading help at a later stage in the writing process.

✔ Make sure children do not see looking up their errors in a dictionary as some kind of punishment or penalty. You can make it a positive activity by keeping the task to a manageable size and by providing help when needed.

Developing a spelling curriculum

The need to plan

A spelling curriculum tells a school and a teacher what to teach and how to teach it. Some objectives are mandated by government and society; others we plan according to the needs of the children and the subjects we teach. If we do not articulate the desired outcomes for education, we cannot effectively plan to make sure they are achieved.

The curriculum will act as a framework on which we can build our year's work. While the basic structure and content will be the same for everyone, each teacher can develop short- and long-term plans to integrate word-level work into the classroom program.

You can base such a school curriculum on the three prerequisites for learning described earlier (see p. 16):

✔ Purpose: why we bother to learn
✔ Information: what we need to know to be successful
✔ Practice: repetition to make skills automatic

Objective	Implementation
Purpose Writing is the only purpose for learning to spell. It is fundamental to spelling instruction that its prime objective is to help children to construct words they need for their own writing. This presupposes that children will have writing that they want and need to do. Children should have many opportunities to set their own purposes for writing. Then they will need to learn about spelling to fulfil their own goals. There is nothing as motivating as self-interest. Writing gives spelling meaning. Meaning is what makes it possible to learn. It is also what makes it worthwhile to bother.	Establish a writers' workshop atmosphere in the classroom, in which children are encouraged to take risks, and are not penalized for making mistakes. Teach the drafting process, in which spelling has its own focus at the appropriate time. Make writing a part of every subject throughout the day. Engage children in the fun of playing with words and finding out about their history and origins. Words are interesting for their own sake and worthy of study. Children should look forward to and enjoy a spelling lesson.

Objective	Implementation
Information This is the content of the curriculum, the topics for our spelling lessons. Once we have decided on the significant patterns and concepts to teach, we can make a sequence for instruction. This will be just a guideline, as spelling is not a sequential subject. However, it can be helpful for each teacher to have an idea of what children have learned before, and what can be left until later years. The list will also provide continuity throughout the child's school life. Each teacher can use the relevant list to plan spelling lessons for the year. The list can also become an assessment checklist for each child, a growing list of what each child knows and is able to do.	List spelling patterns that children need. Categorize the patterns according to sound, function, meaning and word-building. Sequence each category in order of difficulty and suggested sequence of teaching. Divide the list according to what will be taught each year. This will provide a scope-and-sequence chart that each teacher can use as a starting-point for planning. Be prepared to adapt the scope and sequence to the abilities of individual children. Use children's own writing to gauge where they fit and what level of instruction is appropriate.
Practice There are two kinds of practice that children need in order to become familiar with spelling patterns and adept at using them. – First, they need enough examples to be able to recognize a pattern, and enough repetitions of using it to be able to construct their own words as needed. – Second, they need to engage in many different kinds of writing on a daily basis, in order to make using the patterns automatic for them. This will bring them full circle, back to writing as the major motivation for learning more about words and spellings.	Teach a concept using the four-step lesson plan. Provide practice exercises to help children become familiar with using the pattern for constructing words. Provide time daily for personal writing, at which time children write on topics and in modes and styles of their own choice. Plan for teacher-directed writing activities throughout the day. Through these, you can make sure children learn about and engage in many different kinds of writing for different purposes and audiences.

Lifelong learning

When these three conditions — purpose, information and practice — are present, children have their best chance of learning to spell. Not only that, they will see spelling as a tool for writing and a way of learning more about our language and how it can be used. This in turn will contribute to their growth as readers and writers.

A teaching methodology that focuses on pattern recognition and word-building will also give children problem-solving strategies that will enable them to continue their spelling learning throughout their lives. This lifelong learning is the most valuable outcome we can aim for in school.

Index